MW00562136

BUSTED!

Police and Public Safety Ethical Decision-Making

What Psychologists, Mental Health Professionals, and LE Professionals Need to Know

STEPHEN F. CURRAN, Ph.D., ABPP

TOWSON, MD

Copyright © 2020 by Stephen F. Curran, Ph.D., ABPP

All rights reserved. No part of this publication may be reproduced, distributed or transmitted in any form or by any means, including photocopying, recording, or other electronic or mechanical methods, without the prior written permission of the publisher, except in the case of brief quotations embodied in critical reviews and certain other noncommercial uses permitted by copyright law. For permission requests, write to the author, addressed "Permissions" at curran@greensidepsych.org

Publisher, Greenside Psychological Associates, Inc.

Book Layout ©2020 Editor -Wendy Dean, Owner/Publisher The Omnibus Publishing

Cover Design by Alina Zenn, Zennstudio.com

Ordering Information:

Quantity sales. Special discounts are available on quantity purchases by corporations, associations, and others. For details, contact the "Special Sales Department" at the email address above.

Busted! Police and Public Safety Ethical Decision-Making What Psychologists, Mental Health Professionals and LE Professionals Need to Know --1st ed.

Library of Congress Control Number: 2020913126

ISBN 978-1-7354150-0-0 / Kindle 978-1-7354150-1-7

Contents

Acknowledgments

I appreciate the editorial comments provided by my colleague of over 35 years, Marc J. Tabackman, Ph.D. Also, I thank Robert D. Porter for his editorial feedback. Finally, thank you to my daughter and cheerleader, who lit the ignition switch to complete this book, Mary Claire Curran.

Finally, I have had many experiences that each could lead to a book. However, it is the experiences derived from listening to those who take the 9-1-1 call and to the firefighter, paramedic, and/or police officer who are dispatched to a scene that I especially thank for their service. I add to that list the group of men and women often forgotten. Those, who 24/7 provide custody and security for offenders having committed crimes. To the above and their families that support them I thank you.

Introduction
Why the book?

My goals in writing this book have evolved since inception. The idea for the book has been percolating for the past ten years. Yet, as with most of us, there are changing priorities that put some tasks on the back burner. I became re-energized when, so often, it seemed other writings addressing ethical decision making left me wanting more concrete answers. We psychologists and other mental health professionals must have a framework within which to approach our decisions about what constitutes an ethical and responsible decision versus the alternative. The frameworks are useful but sometimes lacking in specificity. I am not prone to scream at a book, but I suspect that you also have had the experience of wanting resources to be more direct. Here is an example. A recent article in the National Psychologist posed the dilemma of treating someone with a sex addiction that may have involved child pornography (Lawson, Tempelmeyer and Hays (2020). The decision-making process as to professional responsibility for reporting left the reader with a wishy-washy "be thoughtful" description. The authors are credited for clearly stating their intent in writing the article, "Our purpose in writing this piece is to clarify the conflict that a therapist faces when a patient reveals this type of information and not to provide an answer to the dilemma." Why no clear opinion? Could I be more direct in writing a book? I hope you conclude that clear guidance has been provided for many dilemmas.

If you seek resources about ethical framework issues, but not necessarily solutions, there are many already penned. For example, *Ethical Practice in Forensic Psychology, A Guide for Mental Health Professionals* (Second Edition) by Bush, Connell and Denney (2020) may be useful although distinct from this book. You will not find the words police or firefighter, or conditions relevant to police and public safety in the Bush et al book.

Consider the following perspective I used in approaching *Busted! Police and Public Safety Ethical Decision-Making*. In 2014 I was asked to chair the annual, pre-APA convention conference of the Division 18 section of Police and Public Safety Psychologists. The theme was "Reaching Across the Aisle." As with any professional group we seem to see the world through a narrow lens. Those of us in the field of Police and Public Safety Psychology sometimes believe the problems faced by police officers, firefighters, paramedics, correctional officers, and dispatchers are so unique that not much can be learned from other disciplines. Thus, I brought together presenters from the Airline Pilots Association, National Football League, Military, and the National Security Agency. Their programs were generalizable to attendees and provided innovative approaches to supporting and sustaining the mental health of their constituents. Similarly, I want to present the reader some perspectives not previously considered. Specifically, business ethics is one area from which we can learn much.

Another dynamic that fueled my writing this book is having acquired over 40 years of experience in the field. If I have not learned much in that time, then when? I have encountered numerous ethical challenges during my career as well as observed the decision making of my colleagues. The latter group comprise some very disappointing decisions from which you and I can learn.

So lets start with a bit about me. No need to dwell on education or academic research on proxemics and violence (Curran et al, 1978) while also actively involved in psychopharmacology (Savage et al, 1976 and Curran and Savage, 1976) and medical device development. The pivotal moment relevant to this book occurred when, at the encouragement of a Major in the Maryland State Police, I attended my first meeting of the Police Psychological Services Section of the International Association of Chiefs of Police (IACP). The annual conference was held in Louisville, Kentucky in October 1989. The police psychologists' group had just become a "section" of IACP having started as a committee a few years prior. In the room was a round table with about ten chairs. I was the youngest in attendance at the age of 39. Among attendees was the father of clinical police psychology, James Shaw, Ph.D. from Olympia, Washington. Dr. Shaw became my mentor. The group was most instrumental in my development as a police psychologist. I went through office holder ranks and became Chair for a two-year term from 1994 to 1996. The 1990's were particularly important to the growth of police psychology and impacts upon chiefs of police and administrators of police and public safety agencies. This time frame had unparalleled success in growing police administration practices that incorporated psychological factors with guidelines on topics of peer support, preemployment screening, fitness for duty and officer involved shootings. As a result of the respect by the police chiefs for the section's guidelines, the section grew considerably with 100+ members by 2000 and today over 200 members. The Police Psychological Services Section became the "go-to" professional organization during the 1990s and 2000s. I have remained active in the Police Psychological Services Section, having not missed an annual IACP conference since my first meeting in 1989.

With the preceding comments as to why the book has been written and the snapshot about me, let's get into the subject matter!

CHAPTER 1

Business Ethics: An Introduction

We each know the difference, right? There is doing what is ethical, then there is doing what is legal, and then there is doing what is moral. Let's spend this chapter on business ethics to set the foundation for discussions throughout the book.

Used with permission: ID 160765305 © Boris15 | Dreamstime.com

The generally accepted definition for business ethics, also called corporate ethics, is a form of applied ethics or professional ethics that examines the ethical and moral principles and problems that arise in a business environment. Business ethics applies to all aspects of business conduct on behalf of both individuals and the entire company.

Law Enforcement, Emergency Services and Associated Public Safety Components

We as psychologists and other mental health professionals do not operate in a vacuum. Our services to agencies are impacted by the business ethics of the organization. Have you conceptualized the police agency, for example, as a business? What is their product? Who are the consumers of their services? Who comprise the Board of Directors i.e., to whom does the agency report? You may be asking yourself, "How does that affect me?" I would say, PLENTY!

Let's take a look at the manner of actions (below) executed in the business environment. These are not absolute constructs but useful when thinking about how an organization impacts your ethical decision making. How often do you assess the business ethics of the organization for whom you provide services? Are you so eager for the business that you accept the police agency as an unquestionable authority on any given topic? How often do you conduct a self-assessment of your own business practices?

I offer the following police practice as an instructive example for not losing sight of psychological ethical standards. Do you recall the advent of cell phone cameras? The first introduction was in Japan in May, 1999. The worldwide use of the camera phone exploded the past 20 years. Who could live without one? Citizens who were suspected of violating a law certainly could not live without one. The result was police would routinely take the cell phone from someone under investigation regardless of the severity of the law suspected of having been violated. Also, police were often seizing the phones from bystanders recording a police incident. This police practice was not uncommon across the United States (and elsewhere). I will bet that the agency or agencies to whom you provided psychological services engaged in this practice as well. Even attorneys representing law enforcement agencies supported the practice. How did this occur when any reasonable non-law enforcement person (the general public) knew "this can't be right." In a short time frame a case ended up at the Supreme Court of the United States. Was the decision of the nine justices a close call? Did the Supreme Court side with law enforcement? No, the decision was a resounding 9 – 0 that the police practice was unlawful.

The 2014 Supreme Court decided that phones can't be searched without a warrant (Riley v. California). The decision highlights how far apart police executives sometimes are from the citizens the agencies are to serve. If law enforcement operated more like private businesses, would they have been more ethically aware?

The below categories provide an overview of the intersection between actions and results. I will make references to the below factors as I proceed in this and subsequent chapters.

Teleological	Actions are judged as ethical or unethical based on results
Egoism	Actions are judged on the consequences to one's self. Maximizing self-interest is the goal.
Utilitarianism	Actions are based on the consequence to "others" – create the greatest good for the greatest number.
Deontological	Actions are judged as ethical or unethical based on rights of others and the intentions of the actor. Individuals are the means and not the ends. Don't judge the consequences.
Justice	Actions are judged on the fairness shown to those affected.
Relativism	Actions are judged as ethical or unethical based on subjective factors that may vary from individual to individual; group to group; and culture to culture.

No Knock Warrants which has allowed police officers to enter a residence without warning and identification.

The **Militarization of Police** as manifested in the deployment of tanks, wearing of tactical, combat ready uniforms, and weapons.

There are other decisions made by police agencies that are equally as high profile as the cell phone confiscation (see sidebar). Each reflects the business ethics of the agency.

Further, the teleological decision making has profound impacts upon law enforcement's primary customer – citizens. Ask your department about what happened to Community Oriented Policing? Ask any person from a minority group about Stop and Frisk and "I Can't Breathe". These are applications of business ethics that are not always fully appreciated.

Here is another to consider from the front page of USA TODAY, "Prosecutors and police agencies fail to track officer misconduct and frequently circumvent Supreme Court "Brady" rules." The headline of the October 17, 2019 story by Steve Reilly and Mark Nichols read, **"Hundreds of police officers have been labeled liars. Some still help send people to prison."**

The reporters found from their investigation that:

- Thousands of people have faced criminal charges or gone to prison based in part on testimony from law enforcement officers deemed to have credibility problems by their bosses or by prosecutors.
- At least 300 prosecutors' offices across the nation are not taking steps necessary to comply with the Supreme Court mandates. These places do not have a list tracking dishonest or otherwise untrustworthy officers.
- In many places that keep lists, police and prosecutors refuse to make them public, making it impossible to know whether they are following the law.

Others keep lists that are incomplete. USA TODAY identified at least 1,200 officers with proven histories of lying and other serious misconduct who had not been flagged by prosecutors. Of those officers, 261 were specifically disciplined for dishonesty on the job.

The authors noted the number of "killings by police" in cities such as Ferguson, Baltimore and Chicago had led to departments to "crack down" on problem police officers. If accurate that would be a step forward. However, does that fit with your reality?

The deontological business ethics of some, but not all, police agencies are important to consider when choosing to work with an agency and what impacts these have for you providing those services. Here is another element to business ethics. Have you ever noticed how often the "Police Officer of the Year" seems to be a harbinger of bad things to emerge about that officer? Similarly, the Sports Illustrated magazine cover has often been cited as a jinx to a professional athlete's career (Smith, 2016). There are numerous examples of this "fall" with subsequent years of poor performance or off-field transgressions. This phenomenon is not limited to athletes or psychologists for that matter. Here is a case study of one of the most heralded banks throughout the past 15 years. The bank successfully navigated the 2008-2009 recession and emerged larger (through acquisition) and respected by industry peers and the customers the bank served. We might call the bank an organization at the top of its game! Their shareholder gains were not surpassed by any of their competitors. What could possibly go wrong for such an organization?

The Wells Fargo Bank Scandal

My purpose in presenting this example is having no personal beef with Wells Fargo Bank. When I review what the various Schools of Business are talking about, I often learn much more than when reading psychological journals. I believe you will agree that Stanford's School of Business and Harvard's School of Business would be credible sources for analyses of what occurs in industry. Thus, when the scandal at the Wells Fargo Bank was hitting the major press outlets and evening news I reflected, "How could this happen?" The "go to" sources for commentary and academic study were those prominent institutions mentioned above. A brilliant analysis was written by Brian Tayan of Stanford's School of Business (Tayan, 2019). Mr. Tayan provides the history of the company through its mission statements and other sources. Wells Fargo prided itself on Vision and Values. The vision of Wells Fargo was "to satisfy our customers' needs and help them succeed financially." Mr.

Tayan cited how Wells Fargo was a business where "we strive to be recognized by our stakeholders as setting the standard among the world's great companies for integrity and principled performance. This is more than just doing the right thing. We also have to do it in the right way."

Southern California became the epicenter during 2013 where rumblings began about Wells Fargo employees engaged in aggressive sales tactics. Initially, about 30 employees were fired because they were opening new accounts and issuing debit or credit cards all without customers knowledge. The scandal grew when we learned of a pattern of branch managers who were setting quotas for selling bank products such as credit cards. If an employee did not reach the daily sales goal, that shortage was added to the next day's sales goal. The financial incentives to employees at Wells Fargo were powerful, with personal bankers receiving bonuses around 20 percent of their base salary. Tellers as well were able to boost their salary by 3 percent.

Wells Fargo seemed to have lost its way to maintaining integrity and principled performance. The damage was done to its reputation. There are no dollar figures to place on reputation. The financial hit taken by Wells Fargo would, on the surface, seem huge - $15 million to settle a lawsuit for practices over a five-year time frame. The amount was minuscule when considering the number of Wells Fargo customers. The impacts upon the organization were numerous, including over 5,000 employees losing their jobs. In the end though, the greatest impact was to Wells Fargo's reputation. At the end of 2019 the bank ranked #10 of the top ten on dividend payouts to shareholders. That drop from the top of the heap to #10 was attributable to their diminished reputation.

Mr. Tayan provides an analysis of factors that went wrong at Wells Fargo Bank with "values" not aligned with behaviors at the top. Although effective component groups (such as, Human Resources, Legal, and Risk Management) were in place, the organization was not adept at recognizing the problem.

What are your values as a professional and how do these conform to the public safety agency to whom you provide services? This chapter may well be worth your time re-reading after the next chapters. Also, the below will become a familiar refrain.

CHAPTER 2

Principles of Psychologists and Code of Conduct

Psychologists are duty bound to adhere to professional standards. That statement may seem obvious, yet serves as an important reminder as we conduct our professional services to organizations and individuals. The focus now is to look at General Principles cited by the American Psychological Association (APA) and without delving into each specific Ethical Standard.

General Principles, as opposed to Ethical Standards, are aspirational in nature. Their intent is to guide and inspire psychologists toward the very highest ethical ideals of the profession.

> *"General Principles, in contrast to Ethical Standards, do not represent obligations and should not form the basis for imposing sanctions. Relying upon General Principles for either of these reasons distorts both their meaning and purpose"* (APA, 2017, page 5).

The following principles are brought to your attention for reflection and self-assessment as we proceed in considering challenges across domains of police psychology including assessment, organizational consultation, and treatment related ethical challenges. These principles are operating in the background of our daily professional lives. We must be attentive to these regularly and not just when faced squarely with a dilemma. The following quote from a memo to all Department of Defense Personnel on August 4, 2017 by then Secretary of Defense, James Mattis, Retired General, highlights that in order to be ready to do what is right we must train and prepare. General Mattis wrote:,

> *"To ensure each of us is ready to do what is right, without hesitation,when ethical dilemmas arise, we must train and prepare ourselves and our subordinates. Our prior reflection and our*

choice to live by an ethical code will reinforce what we stand for, so we remain morally strong, especially in the face of adversity."

The reader is encouraged to consider the implications upon our daily conduct while rendering services to individuals and organizations. We have to "train up" for this so that we will make ethical and responsible decisions. The following are from the APA website.

- **Principle A: Beneficence and Nonmaleficence**

"Psychologists strive to benefit those with whom they work and take care to do no harm. In their professional actions, psychologists seek to safeguard the welfare and rights of those with whom they interact professionally and other affected persons, and the welfare of animal subjects of research. When conflicts occur among psychologists' obligations or concerns, they attempt to resolve these conflicts in a responsible fashion that avoids or minimizes harm. Because psychologists' scientific and professional judgments and actions may affect the lives of others, they are alert to and guard against personal, financial, social, organizational, or political factors that might lead to misuse of their influence. Psychologists strive to be aware of the possible effect of their own physical and mental health on their ability to help those with whom they work."

What are the implications from this Principal?

- Is your risk aversion impacted by economics?
- Are the consumers (agencies) of our services being considered in our decision making?
- Are we looking out for the best interests of the firefighters, police officers and others we serve?

- **Principle B: Fidelity and Responsibility**

"Psychologists establish relationships of trust with whom

they work. They are aware of their professional and scientific responsibilities to society and to the specific communities in which they work. Psychologists uphold professional standards of conduct, clarify their professional roles and obligations, accept appropriate responsibility for their behavior, and seek to manage conflicts of interest that could lead to exploitation or harm. Psychologists consult with, refer to, or cooperate with other professionals and institutions to the extent needed to serve the best interests of those with whom they work. They are concerned about the ethical compliance of their colleagues' scientific and professional conduct. Psychologists strive to contribute a portion of their professional time for little or no compensation or personal advantage."

Implications:

- Am I collecting data on a routine basis about my decision making of an applicant's psychological stability and suitability?
- Am I monitoring adverse impacts upon minority groups related to preemployment and fitness evaluations?

• **Principle C: Integrity**

"Psychologists seek to promote accuracy, honesty, and truthfulness in the science, teaching, and practice of psychology. In these activities, psychologists do not steal, cheat or engage in fraud, subterfuge, or intentional misrepresentation of fact. Psychologists strive to keep their promises to avoid unwise or unclear commitments. In situations in which deception may be ethically justifiable to maximize benefits and minimize harm, psychologists have a serious obligation to consider the need for, the possible consequences of, and their responsibility to correct any resulting mistrust or other harmful effects that arise from the use of such techniques."

Implications:

– Is there favoritism in the selection of a certain applicant?
– Are my invoices accurately reflecting services rendered?

• **Principle D: Justice**

"Psychologists recognize that fairness and justice entitle all persons to access to and benefit from the contributions of psychology and to equal quality in the processes, procedures, and services being conducted by psychologists. Psychologists exercise reasonable judgment and take precautions to ensure that their potential biases, the boundaries of their competence, and the limitations of their expertise do not lead to or condone unjust practices."

Implications:

– Do you benefit from being provided background data?
– Are there implicit and explicit biases impacting your decision making?
– Do you educate background investigators about anchoring bias?

• **Principle E: Respect for People's Rights and Dignity**

"Psychologists respect the dignity and worth of all people, and the rights of individuals to privacy, confidentiality, and self-determination. Psychologists are aware that special safe guards may be necessary to protect the rights and welfare of persons or communities whose vulnerabilities impair autonomous decision making. Psychologists are aware of and respect cultural, individual, and role differences, including those based on age, gender identity, race, ethnicity, culture, national origin, religion, sexual orientation, disability, language, and socioeconomic status, and consider these factors when working with members of such groups. Psychologists try to eliminate the effect on their work of biases based on those factors, and they do not knowingly participate in or condone activities of others based upon such prejudices.

Implications:

- Do you fairly assess public safety personnel where English is the second language?
- Women should never be firefighters! NEVER you say! Really?
- Do you have data that backs up thinking applicants in same sex relationships are unsuitable?

CHAPTER 3

Introduction to Police and Public Safety Psychology

Photo used with permission: ID 84739615 © Adonis1969 | Dreamstime.com

My intuition tells me that if you are reading this book then you are:

a. Experienced in the field of psychology, social work and counseling
b. Hold an advanced degree and curious about the field
c. An academician at a Criminal Justice program
d. An inquisitive undergraduate or graduate student seeking to sort out career opportunities or even better yet,
e. An administrator, Fire Chief, Police Chief or other public safety services official.

Here is when I admit my lack of objectivity. The field of Police and Public Safety Psychology is an awesome field. Do you derive satisfaction from teaching but not as a full-time instructor? Do you love counseling but not all day long, every day of the week? Do you like making assessments but not day in and day out having to write reports? If yes, then this field may be a good blend of tasks for you. Police Psychology and all of the related public safety fields that have evolved provide opportunities to serve and lead. There are at least 57 proficiencies where psychologists and mental health professionals have opportunities. I am going to bet if you are the curious reader perhaps you can name no more than five domains? (I already provided three). The field is quite diverse!

Current breadth of Police & Public Safety Psychology

The following table contains a partial list of activities that fall within four core domains:

- Assessment
- Intervention
- Operational
- Consultation

Some of these activities require specific education and licensure requirements while others, such as those within consultation and operations, do not. Each domain needs greater research thus opportunities exist for researchers.

Assessment Domain

Job Analysis
Post Offer of Employment Psychological Assessment
Return to Work Evaluation
Test Development
Assessment Centers

Intervention Domain

Individual Therapy
Family, Group, and Marital Therapy
Substance Abuse Recovery
Critical Incident Interventions
Critical Incident Counseling
Wellness Programs
Life Coaching

Operational Domain

Psychological Autopsy for Case Resolution

Psychological Intelligence

Operational Training

Threat Assessment

Consulting Domain

Organizational Development

Executive Consultation

Supervisor Consultation

The four domains and 57 proficiencies of police psychology were agreed to by the three predominant organizations to which psychologists, graduate criminal justice related programs, researchers and other mental health professionals belong (Aumiller et al, 2008)[4]. I discussed the IACP, Police Psychological Services Section in Chapter 1. Today, there are over 200 members of which the predominant professional group are psychologists. The core benefit to the IACP section is that, compared to most professional groups, the percentage of members attending each year's conference typically exceeds 50%. Another benefit is providing for face to face interactions with 16,000 police chiefs from around the globe who attend the annual conference.

Another group is the Society for Police and Criminal Psychology (SPCP). This organization has a greater influence of academicians and researchers as the composition of its membership. The organization self-describes as being

---

4 For the complete listing of the 57 proficiencies see Appendix A as adapted from Aumiller, G.S., Corey, D., Allen, S., Brewster, J., Cuttler, M., Gupton, H. and Honig, A. Defining the Field of Police Psychology: Core Domains & Proficiencies. *J Police Crim Psych* 22, 65–76

"an eclectic professional organization that encourages the scientific study of police and criminal psychology and the application of scientific knowledge to problems in criminal justice. It focuses on law enforcement, judicial, and corrections elements in criminal justice. Members of the Society study the full range of human behaviors, motivations, and actions within the framework of the criminal justice system. Consequently, the Society encourages input from psychologists, social workers, psychiatrists, lawyers, police officers, corrections personnel, and other professionals concerned with the criminal justice system." (SPCP).

The third recognized group is Division 18 of the American Psychological Association (APA). Division 18 is diverse Psychologists in Public Service with distinct components that include Veterans Administration Psychologists, Community and State Hospitals, Serious Mental Illness, Health, Indian Affairs, Criminal Justice in addition to Police and Public Safety Psychology. The APA sub-section of Police and Public Safety has about 300 members who identify as part of the group, but attendance at annual APA pre-convention workshops is rather low as a percentage of division members. There are two fledgling professional groups to mention, although neither has yet to gain prominence in the field. They are the Fire Service Psychological Association and a psychological services group of the National Sheriff's Association.

The "politics" within organizations are not unique to psychologists and mental health professionals that serve police, emergency services, fire and rescue, and corrections. Organizational dynamics are often important when pursuing appropriate ethical decisions. In the opinion of this author, the IACP section of Police Psychological Services has evolved to a point where it may possibly be losing sight of its goals – a case of traditional blurring of goals. The mission of the group is to serve police chiefs, although some would opine that the group has become centered on profession interests. Let me compare the dynamics to another group of IACP. The Police Physicians Section of IACP, which evolved later than the psychologist section. Early on, the Police Physicians Section aligned itself with the American College of Occupational and Environmental Medicine (ACOEM)[5]. This strategic decision has yielded benefits to members of ACOEM. The documents produced by the Police Physicians Section are published through ACOEM and not IACP. On all medical matters related to police, fire and related high-risk occupations this section is the recognized professional group. The possibility for the APA's Division 18 sub-group to become similarly positioned is not too late. This commentary is meant for the reader to reflect on the multiple levels where ethical conflicts can emerge. Organization structural factors often impact the role, responsibilities and conduct of its members. Reflecting on business ethics, the actions of some professional groups may reflect egoism.

The impacts from the organizational factors have left wide open opportunities to assist both police, public safety agencies and the communities served. While self-serving professional focus has been occurring, so have the following, although sadly not addressed by organized police psychology:

- Excessive Use of Force Impacts on Minorities (See Chapter 9 for discussion)
- Texting related Motor Vehicle Crashes
- Pedestrian/Biking deaths 25% of all deaths on roads
- Child exploitation
- Alcohol involved crashes
- Fire setting
- Domestic Violence

5 Full disclosure, the author is an Associate Member of the ACOEM and an office holder of the Behavioral Health Section of the ACOEM.

The list goes on. We, regardless of professional affiliation, have unique skills and perspectives that may contribute to society. For an overview and discussion of the diverse roles that psychologists provide see Trompetter (2011).

CHAPTER 4

Competence

char • la • tan
/SHärlədən, 'SHärlətn/
Noun
1: *charlatans* harming their patients with dubious procedures
2: one making usually showy pretenses to knowledge or ability: FRAUD, FAKER. (Merriam-Webster, 2020).

Learn to pronounce this word since you will run into this person often!

USED WITH PERMISSION: ID 164975670 © AHASOFT | DREAMSTIME.COM

More than once during my career I have encountered the psychologist who defends his or her procedures with, I have been doing this for 20+ year, as if with the passage of time we become more competent. Further, doing something wrong for 20+ years does not make it right.

APA Section 2.01 Boundaries of Competence states that, "(a) Psychologists provide services, teach, and conduct research with populations and in areas only within the boundaries of their competence, based on their education, training, supervised experience, consultation, study, or professional experience. (b) Where scientific or professional knowledge in the discipline of psychology establishes that an understanding of factors associated with age, gender and gender identity, race, ethnicity, culture, national origin, religion, sexual orientation, disability, language, or socioeconomic status is essential for effective implementation of their services or research, psychologists have or obtain the training, experience, consultation, or supervision necessary to ensure the competence of their services, or they make appropriate referrals, except as provided in Standard 2.02, Providing Services in Emergencies" (APA, 2017).

Case Example: The Baltimore Police Department

THE BALTIMORE SUN

Firm that screens police investigated

Permission from the Baltimore Sun Media. All Rights Reserved

In 2015, soon after the high profile, in-custody death of Freddie Gray, and the riots in Baltimore, the investigative reporting conducted by the Baltimore Sun revealed procedures by a psychological services firm that suggested illegal and unethical practices. The firm had been providing a range of psychological services to the Baltimore Police Department (BPD) since the 1970's. Once the radio and television outlets picked up the Baltimore Sun story, the City of Baltimore terminated the contract with the firm.

What happened to the principal psychologist of the firm? A few years elapsed before the Board of Examiners for Maryland Psychologists took action that only consisted in prohibiting the psychologist from conducting police related assessments (Maryland Board of Examiners, Case Number 2016-126, February 2, 2018). The psychologist did not lose his license. The impact of years of negligent psychological assessment practices continues to have consequences upon the citizens of Baltimore and the Baltimore Police Department. These impacts have yet to be fully recognized by these constituents.

What were the practices? In this chapter I will address only the assessment component utilized by the psychological services firm. The boundary violations of fitness for duty and counseling services will be discussed later.

The assessment protocol consisted of one psychological measure that was administered prior to the Conditional Offer of Employment (COE), in violation of Equal Employment Opportunity Commission (EEOC) enforcement of the ADA regulations (EEOC, 1995). After the COE there may have been the completion of a non-standardized version of an objective inventory or a few selected items from that inventory.

In addition, projective testing was administered at the time of the face to face interview. Among projective tests were the Draw-A-Person. To date, there are no data to support the validity and reliability of that measure in the selection of police officers. The Board of Examiners findings stated,

> *"The Respondent, however, did not provide any data or documentation, other than his personal experience, to substantiate that a "sentence completion" or "draw-a-person" test had any relevance or reliability to evaluating police applicants."* (page 5 of Findings of Fact).

The drawing was completed during an interview lasting no longer than twenty minutes. This meant that a psychologist from this firm could conduct 20+ evaluations per day. The transcript from the Board of Examiners indicates that the psychologist defended the procedures based in part in having read books online. In addition, the psychologist had not ever attended a professional meeting relevant to professional police psychology. For this psychologist, Competence = Years of doing the wrong thing.

The reader is reminded that APA Standard 2.03 Maintaining Competence requires, "Psychologists undertake ongoing efforts to develop and maintain their competence." Some states have specific regulations that impose the required number of continuing education credits. In many respects, having a government entity impose requirements that may foster competence speaks poorly about professionals not self-regulating their scope of practice. However, more states seem to need specific requirements for psychologists to achieve in order to engage in assessments and maintain competence to conduct psychological evaluations of police and related public safety candidates.

The fall-out from years of negligent hiring is further exemplified by actions of The Gun Trace Task Force (GTTF) unit of the Baltimore Police Department. Here are the prominent facts:

- Officers in the elite Gun Trace Task Force carried out a campaign of robbery and extortion, often targeted suspected drug dealers. The officers allegedly pocketed hundreds of thousands of dollars they discovered while searching the homes and cars of alleged criminals and some innocent civilians.
- The federal corruption case spread beyond Baltimore. A Philadelphia officer was charged with helping distribute drugs stolen by members of the GTTF.

There were 12 officers convicted and sentenced with at least one additional case pending as of 2020.

"The ringleader in the GTTF corruption case was sentenced to 25 years in federal prison, followed by three years of supervised release. The judge split the difference between the 20 years one defendant (Jenkins) asked for and the 30 years the government sought. The judge refused a more lenient sentence, citing, in part, Jenkins' role as a drug dealer with a badge. "He's admitted to ... putting poison in our community when he should

have been protecting the community ... deterrence is important," U.S. District Judge Catherine C. Blake said at sentencing" (Baltimore Sun, June 7, 2018).

The Commissioner of the Baltimore Police Department responded to the criminal convictions, but unlikely has yet to recognize past and current deficiencies in his department with respect to incompetent psychological evaluations. The Commissioner stated in October 2019, "I recognize how vital and important it is to the department and the court to understand the circumstances that allowed the GTTF's activities to take place and go on for so long," (Baltimore Police announce outside investigation into the Gun Trace Task Force scandal, October 23, 2019, The Baltimore Sun).

Personnel problems begin with negligent hiring practices. Is there a causal connection between negligent hiring and rotten police officers? Identifying from competent preemployment psychological assessments, the 90% or more of suitable candidates is the easy part. The more difficult challenge is identifying the small group of personality disordered, impulse driven and rule-violating candidates. These are the candidates who, if hired, are more likely to engage in the conduct manifested by GTTF unit members. You may be questioning that perhaps it's a stretch to link the conduct of GTTF members to the sub-par preemployment assessment. I would disagree but acknowledge that factors of inadequate supervision do come into play. Recall Wells Fargo Bank. Arrests over values lead to the lost integrity of an organization.

While a number of factors impacted the ongoing GTTF members criminal conduct, you may agree on the following case. There was the BPD case where a recent academy graduate and still on probation, since a recent graduate, was caught in prostitution where the officer was pimping his wife. Do you suspect that the preemployment evaluation should have been able to identify the negative enduring personality pathology of this officer?

Remember Chapter 2 about business ethics? The psychological services described above occurred in an environment of business practices that condoned and even encouraged misconduct. Any one of us can imagine wanting to please our "customer", the police agency, but fail to consider how far are we willing to place standards on the proverbial shelf. An agency such as the Baltimore Police Department benefited from low preemployment evaluation fees, few applicant rejections and an overall vendor who would comply with their requirements. Do you think the Baltimore Police Department didn't know what the psychological services firm was doing? A year prior to the media reporting on the firm, I had the occasion to ask a representative of the Baltimore Police Department's contracts division, "Wouldn't BPD want to pay out less because of fewer civil suits against the department for excessive force and other complaints by paying more for competent psychological preemployment evaluations?" The staggering response was (paraphrased), "We don't care since the pay outs do not come from our (BPD) budget, they come from someone else's budget." Can you imagine private industry functioning in a similar maladaptive manner?

This pattern is not unique to the Baltimore Police Department. Similar examples across the United States occur more frequently than the public is aware. For example, the Minneapolis Police Department (MPD) has had a series of questionable shootings by police officers. An American Public Media report on December 14, 2017 concluded that the examination protocol used by the MPD to examine an officer involved in a questionable shooting, "is less rigorous than best practices nationally and the evaluator lacked the proper license." Further, it pointed out, "Minneapolis has fired some of the most qualified police psychologists in the state, and then turned to a succession of mental health professionals with little or no experience in the field (including the ones most recently selected to continue to perform the exams) (APM, 2017)."

The officer involved in this example had been on the job less than two years. There is little doubt the MPD chose a business model where the impact on the public was considered inconsequential. Other examples include the Cleveland Police Department where the hiring of an officer who shot and killed a 14-year-old will be discussed in Chapter 9.

CHAPTER 5

The Web of Multiple Relationships

3.05 Multiple Relationships

"(a) A multiple relationship occurs when a psychologist is in a professional role with a person and (1) at the same time is in another role with the same person, (2) at the same time is in a relationship with a person closely associated with or related to the person with whom the psychologist has the professional relationship, or (3) promises to enter into another relationship in the future with the person or a person closely associated with or related to the person.

A psychologist refrains from entering into a multiple relationship if the multiple relationship could reasonably be expected to impair the psychologist's objectivity, competence, or effectiveness in performing his or her functions as a psychologist, or otherwise risks exploitation or harm to the person with whom the professional relationship exists" (APA, 2017).

If you have jumped to this chapter in the hopes that the following will be acceptable then stop now and go back to Chapter One. The following are never (there, I said it) acceptable:

a. Conducting a fitness exam on someone you previously treated.
b. Conducting a fitness exam on someone your office mate or anyone within your practice has treated.
c. Provide a rating of impairment in a worker's compensation case on someone you treated.
d. Have a sexual relationship with a client whose partner or spouse is a firefighter, police officer or related public safety personnel OR having a partner known to carry guns.

In case of any confusion, there is never an instance where sexual activity with an active client is acceptable (Standard 10.05).

I have consulted on a few legal cases during my career. The #1 reason being asked as an expert consultant falls within dual relationship violations. These occurred across the United States, so I cannot infer a jurisdictional factor as to why psychologists get into an ethical bind. Sometimes the problem seems to reflect an inability to simply say, "*No*." You may want to accommodate an agency but do not ever allow yourself to become involved in multiple relationships.

Case Example: The Baltimore Police Department (again)

I again refer to the Baltimore based psychological services firm referenced earlier. The firm provided not only preemployment assessments but counseling to officers and their family members as well as fitness for duty of officers. The psychologist would accept a fitness evaluation based on word of mouth from any uniformed supervisor. The officer would typically be found unfit, at which time counseling would begin with another mental health provider within the same office. Counseling might last months to a year or more, at which time another or same provider would find the officer fit to return to work. Does this sound problematic to you? I thought so, and now go to the head of the class.

Summary:

The organizational structure within which you work impacts your decision-making. If you are an employee within the structure, such as a correctional facility, how do you sort through which treatment or assessment services are ethically responsible when your primary assignment relates to inmate services? Other potential conflicts to sort through are those employed with a police or other public safety agency while maintaining an independent private practice. Again, I'll use the correctional facility as an example. Are you able to provide psychotherapy as an independent provider to a correctional officer one day and then the next day write up a report of an observed, excessive use of force by that same officer on an inmate as an employee at the correctional facility? These are important factors to sort out well before you enter these relationships.

CHAPTER 6

Assessment

The range of psychological assessments provided by psychologists to public safety organizations has become the core domain for many psychologists in the field. These are described in greater detail by the author with examples of the spectrum of assessments below (Curran, 2014).

Examples of Psychological Assessments in Police & Public Safety

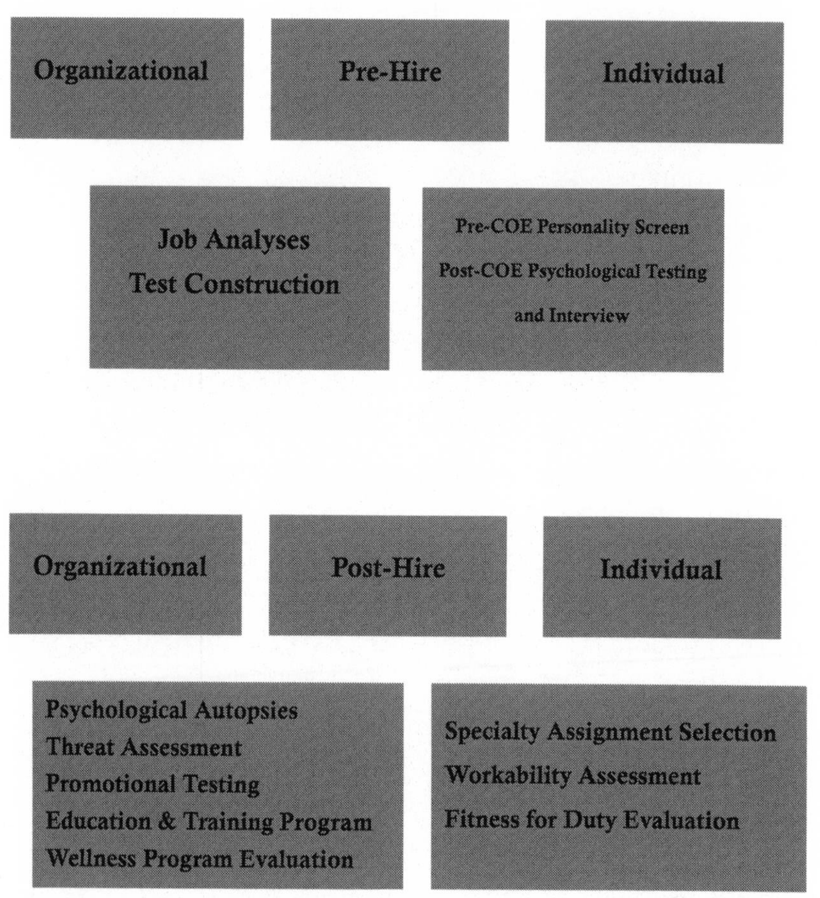

This chapter will review some of the essential elements needed to foster ethical conduct when conducting assessments. The issues are often complex, with distinct challenges depending on evaluations prior to an applicant's hiring as opposed to assessments made after starting on the job. This domain is the employment law component to forensic psychological practice.

Preemployment Assessment

The cornerstone of psychologist service to public safety has been within the preemployment selection phase. The specific application of objective psychological measures to the selection of police officers started to emerge during the 1970s. Among the earliest research projects was a study conducted by Robert Hogan, Ph.D. in the use of the California Psychological Inventory (CPI) (Hogan, 1975). Dr. Hogan's research was the precursor to current, generally accepted domains required of a police officer.

Among the reasons these assessments are valued is candidate attrition, resulting in high costs to recruit and train replacement officers. Deputy Chief Younts from the High Point, North Carolina Fire Department underscored the costs associated with losing 22 firefighters, of which 13 had less than three years on the job, over a three year time frame due to failure to adapt to the firefighter career or due to disobeying rules (Younts, 2003). While the reasons for conducting preemployment evaluations are numerous, the frequency of this component to the hiring process is surprisingly low. The only public safety position with even a minimal collection of data about pre-hire components is the police. The most recent Bureau of Justice Statistics data are contrasting 2003 and 2007 hiring steps by departments, sorted by size of populations served (BJS, 2010). The reader may be surprised to learn that fewer than half of all departments require any type of aptitude test. Further, the report cites that 72% of departments conduct psychological evaluations. The Bureau of Justice Statistics statistics did not specify a definition of what constituted a psychological evaluation, and the qualifications of the examining health care professional. The overall report of 72% is meaningless since was not defined. The 2016 collection of data is not much better. The results are expected to be released sometime in 2020.

Here are the questions asked under the heading "Personal Attributes." The selected department is asked to indicate "yes" or "no" to which components are done as part of hiring.

- Personal interview
- Personality/psychological inventory
- Polygraph exam
- Psychological interview
- Voice stress analyzer
- Written aptitude test
- Analytical/problem-solving ability assessment

The reader is advised to consider the impact of these decisions about survey questions. The decision to not have greater specificity results in less utility of the results. Among these is from a business approach on how effectively are products or services are developed and sold if demographics and spending patterns of potential customers is old data or incomplete data. With this background let's look at the assessment stages, personality testing and post-conditional offer of employment medical evaluation.

1. **Personality Testing – Pre-Conditional Offer of Employment**

The Equal Employment Opportunities Commission (EEOC, 1995) regulations, which implement the ADA, allow for inquiries and tests that occur prior to the Conditional Offer of Employment (COE). Within the behavioral areas this pertains to those behaviors such as domestic violence, violations of laws ranging from speeding citations to texting while driving, and job terminations among others. Elements that are NOT allowed are those inquiries that might lead to a diagnosable condition. Thus, tests that inquire about potential health conditions such as drug dependence or interviews by licensed health care professionals are disallowed. This all may seem uncomplicated. If only that were the case. There has been what a magician might describe as sleight of hand. I am not referring to manual dexterity to confuse a crowd. The sleight of hand I am referring to is the adroitness in deception. The range of how some psychologists have used pre-conditional personality testing to their economic advantage includes:

- some large agencies and even states accepting a "personality measure" as meeting the standard for having a "psychological evaluation (defined below)"
- some departments have a psychologist administer "personality" testing and conduct an interview prior to the COE. One psychologist rationalized the conduct as follows:

"From an agency standpoint, it is more efficient. One could argue that involving a psychologist raises the question of performing a medical inquiry pre-COE. I'm willing to take that risk."

Here is what the psychologist is really saying:

- Forget **Principle A: Beneficence and Nonmaleficence** (page 20), applicants (mostly young) won't object to the procedure. If they do, they label themselves as a potential "troublemaker" that departments won't want to consider for hiring.
- "I can get away with it."

2. **Post-Conditional Offer of Employment Medical Examination**

When we speak of preemployment psychological assessments, most often the procedures relate to the combination of objective psychological testing AND an interview with a licensed, doctoral level psychologist. Let's break down those components of testing and interview.

Testing and Interview

The absence of one element equals no psychological assessment. There are many police and public safety agency representatives who claim to conduct preemployment psychological evaluations of their applicants. When asked if the evaluation is conducted by a doctoral level professional with training in psychometrics and experience in evaluating their specific population, the answer is eerily consistent. The glazed over, "*what*"-expression, followed by the "*I don't know*" response, often occurs. Your challenge, and this is no small task, is to educate departments on this subject.

The department often knows no difference between professional groups nor the education and training between the professional groups. The police administrators do, however, recognize lower fees when they see them. The competent and ethical psychologist is up against those that a) have less education and training and b) will provide the minimal, if not sub-par, assessment protocols. For example, you may think that psychological test publishers already solved part of the problem because their websites and printed materials refer to "qualifications." Surely only a highly trained person would be able to purchase the test. Let me, in my best bellowing voice, holler out, ***Ho, Ho, Ho!*** (yes, that is my Santa impression). Test publishers are in the business of sales, nothing more. Think of the top three tests you use and the publisher/distributor of those tests. Are these companies U.S. based firms listed on the New York Stock Exchange? If you are thinking of firms from whom you purchase the MMPI-2-RF (Pearson), CPI (The Myers-Briggs Company) or IPI-2 (PSI) then the answer is no. Does that come as a surprise? What difference does that make? If you are generating some thoughts about corporate structure impacting values, then you are indeed ahead of many. One of the above referenced companies promotes being a "B Certified Corporation" which sounds impressive. The designation has no legal status, and some would describe the designation as not more than purchasing a diploma.

I was so impressionable and idealistic decades ago when encountering a certain non-psychologist mental health professional in my area, who would give psychological tests to claimants to take home and complete. These were claimants undergoing Independent Medical Evaluations (IMEs). The subsequent report from this referred to provider would either cut and paste segments from a computerized, interpretive report or simply indicate that the results were "pending." I thought that surely the test publisher would want to know about these egregious behaviors of that provider. The test publisher would certainly restrict any further sales to that provider until meeting acceptable standards. Here it comes…***Ho, Ho, Ho!*** No way was the test publisher going to take action. It took me several letters to the publisher to finally let it sink in that this (and other) mental health providers were able to engage in whatever they wanted. As long as they were paid, the publisher had no interest in imposing any restrictions to use their product.

If you are a licensed doctoral level psychologist, you may have thought the level of qualifications needed to purchase test products actually meant something. Think again. If you are a clinical social worker, LPC or other then how do you ethically resolve using measures for which you have not been trained? The selection of law enforcement officers, EMS, Firefighters, Dispatchers and related is no small matter.

These positions require the ultimate in decision making under high stress conditions. The stakes are at the highest level – saving and taking lives!

If you have any doubts about publishers of psychological tests, consider the Case Example #5 described by Lowman, R, L, (Ed) (2006) in the classic, Ethical Practice of Psychology in

Organizations, Second Edition. An Industrial/Organizational (I/O) psychologist, who was a test reviewer of an inventory, discovered an item was mis-keyed. When the psychologist brought the error to the attention of the publishing company's psychologist, the response was far from collegial. The test-publishing company psychologist was verbally abusive to the I/O psychologist for bringing the error to the attention of the company.

There is seemingly no limit to which test products are protected by publishers. Keep this in mind for a moment, the Myers-Briggs Type Indicator (MBTI) is promoted as the most popular personality test in the world. Do I detect a possible chuckle? You must be recalling how your early foundation in psychology was completing a course on tests and measurements where validity and reliability were essential. The distributor, Consulting Psychologists Press, Inc., leads a market in psychological testing worth around $2 billion a year. What have we always known about the MBTI? The measure lacks validity and related psychometric properties (Forbes Magazine 2018). The above factors require vigilance by users of these products such as psychologists and agencies that retain psychologists to conduct assessments.

This chapter has thus far set the parameters for digging into the elements of ethical and responsible assessments. Assessments all begin with informed consent to participate in the evaluation. This is step one. Without a properly constructed consent, the psychologist opens the door to complaints.

3.10 Informed Consent

"(a) When psychologists conduct research or provide assessment, therapy, counseling, or consulting services in person or via electronic transmission or other forms of communication, they obtain the informed consent of the individual or individuals using language that is reasonably understandable to that person or persons except when conducting such activities without consent is mandated by law or governmental regulation or as otherwise provided in this Ethics Code." (APA 2017).

9.03 Informed Consent in Assessments

"(a) Psychologists obtain informed consent for assessments, evaluations, or diagnostic services, as described in Standard 3.10, Informed Consent, except when (1) testing is mandated by law or governmental regulations; (2) informed consent is implied because testing is conducted as a routine educational, institutional, or organizational activity (e.g., when participants voluntarily agree to assessment when applying for a job); or (3) one purpose of the testing is to evaluate decisional capacity. Informed consent includes an explanation of the nature and purpose of the assessment, fees, involvement of third parties, and limits of confidentiality and sufficient opportunity for the client/patient to ask questions and receive answers.

(b) Psychologists inform persons with questionable capacity to consent or for whom testing is mandated by law or governmental regulations about the nature and purpose of the proposed assessment services, using language that is reasonably understandable to the person being assessed." (APA, 2017).

Do you require a signed consent to evaluate?

	Response %	Response Tally
Yes, always	90.5%	86
Sometimes	4.2%	4
No, rarely or never	5.3%	5
		95 answered

You may believe that obtaining an informed consent is a no-brainer. Let me stop you in your thought process to consider some results from a non-scientific survey I conducted of psychologists who provide assessment services to law enforcement agencies (Curran, 2008). These were not rookies new to the field. Nearly 10% of the 95% of respondents never, rarely or sometimes obtain informed consent. I bet you would not have guessed that response rate. The start to any assessment is with consent in which the examinee understands the scope of evaluation, to whom a report of findings be submitted and clearly specifying limits to confidentiality.

The second important component is the assessment protocol. The reader is strongly encouraged to have read and understood at a minimum the following.

- Professional Practice Guidelines for Occupationally Mandated Psychological Evaluations (OMPE). (APA 2018).
- Preemployment Psychological Evaluation Guidelines (IACP, 2014).
- Fitness for Duty Evaluation Guidelines (IACP 2018).

With the above I's dotted and T's crossed, coupled with a signed consent that covers the bases, you may think the coast is clear. However, after you to start the interview, an applicant states mid-way through the evaluation, "I withdraw my consent to release my report to Department XYZ (the prospective employer)[4]." The police officer applicant, for example, has figured out during the interview that you are likely going to render an unfavorable report and thus refuses to permit you to release the information to Department XYZ. The applicant says he will pay for the evaluation instead. What do you do? This is a rare but not uncommon incident.

In this example, the client has signed a consent to the evaluation prior to starting an interview. The consent stated that Department XYZ was your client. You are more than pleased to advise Department XYZ that the applicant rescinded his part of the agreement and does not want a report submitted. The applicant is perhaps so severely personality disordered that the consequences are not appreciated. The applicant's withdrawal

4 A variant to this type of applicant is the one that says, "I plan to sue you if you disqualify me."

of consent to release the report is no different than refusing to submit to the psychological evaluation. How well will a department agree to terms set by an applicant? You cannot foresee all circumstances, but this is one that can serve to foster your cooperative working relationship with Department XYZ. A conversation is needed with the department's contact about some curve balls thrown at you with expectation that the department will rely on your handling the situation and provide payment for your professional services. You can cite the ethical standard that has guided you (3.11).

Can you imagine what would happen to your reputation if police and public safety agencies learned that you accepted payment from an applicant to not submit a report? Recalling Wells Fargo, there is no amount of money that can be placed on reputation once damaged.

Two standards that are helpful to rely upon are:

- **3.11 Psychological Services Delivered to or Through Organizations**

"(a) Psychologists delivering services to or through organizations provide information beforehand to clients and when appropriate those directly affected by the services about (1) the nature and objectives of the services, (2) the intended recipients, (3) which of the individuals are clients, (4) the relationship the psychologist will have with each person and the organization, (5) the probable uses of services provided and information obtained, (6) who will have access to the information, and (7) limits of confidentiality. As soon as feasible, they provide information about the results and conclusions of such services to appropriate persons.
(b) If psychologists will be precluded by law or by organizational roles from providing such information to particular individuals or groups, they so inform those individuals or groups at the outset of the service."

- **9.01 Bases for Assessments**

"(a) Psychologists base the opinions contained in their recommendations, reports, and diagnostic or evaluative statements, including forensic testimony, on information and techniques sufficient to substantiate their findings.
(b) Except as noted in 9.01c, psychologists provide opinions of the psychological characteristics of individuals only after they have conducted an examination of the individuals adequate to support their statements or conclusions. When, despite reasonable efforts, such an examination is not practical, psychologists document the efforts they made and the result of those efforts, clarify the probable impact of their limited information on the reliability and validity of their opinions, and appropriately limit the nature and extent of their conclusions or recommendations.
(c) When psychologists conduct a record review or provide consultation or supervision and an individual examination is not warranted or necessary for the opinion, psychologists explain this and the sources of information on which they based their conclusions and recommendations."

Let's look at the elements of an assessment, now that an informed consent has been obtained and you have applied the above standards to your decision making about how to proceed.

a. Testing protocol – most assessments will require an examinee (applicant or employee) complete at least one valid and reliable measure. The referral question(s) will impact the types of tests administered. As already described above, the preemployment evaluation is a "medical" examination The evaluation will minimally consist of two measures for the purposes of identifying psychopathology as well as normal pathology/suitability. In contrast, an examination for return to work (workability) as opposed to fitness for duty may consist of one measure to establish stability.

b. Environment – Step back and look at your office setting. Is it free of distractions ranging from noise to other environmental influences? I am not making this up but doing your laundry at your home office while conducting an interview seems a poor decision.

c. Observers – the data are clear that you do not nor should you allow third party observers to any evaluation. Among factors that impact an evaluation when conducted with observers are the effects on performance. Bush et al (2020) has pointed out the problems and recommendations for handling observer requests. This element is rarely encountered when conducting preemployment assessments although occurs when job jeopardy fitness evaluations are requested. Note: There are jurisdictions where labor agreements, for example, allow for an observer.

d. Telehealth – APA has guidelines to follow, so refer to them to mitigate against risk (APA, 2013). The practice of telehealth has grown for those rendering counseling services. Be advised that there is no research data to solidly support use of telehealth platforms for assessment purposes. Luxton, Pruitt, and Osenbach (2014) cited that "practitioners would be remiss to simply assume equivalency between in-person and remote administration of psychological assessments." These same authors commented upon the cultural factors where interpersonal connectedness or nonverbal interactions are impacted. An evaluator will need to be prepared to defend their procedures and findings if an evaluation is other than in-person, in office, and face-to-face. Bush, S.S., Connell, M. and Denney, R.L. (2020) noted that while the APA guidelines are useful "...additional empirical investigation is needed to address technological applications of forensic psychological services…" The COVID-19 pandemic will likely be described in future psychology annals as an explosion in the use of telehealth by psychologists and other mental health professionals. The pandemic may well serve as an exception in some assessment cases but without sufficient empirical evidence, whose interests are we serving; our clients? When I have thrown caution to the wind about evaluations that are not done in person, the responses from professionals have approached intense reactions. Some ask, "Why would anyone think there is a difference?" This group maintains that someone throwing caution should do the research and not them. Let's just see how well autonomous cars will gain acceptance if the manufacturers don't do the research to establish safety and equivalency to or better than live drivers. Another group throws out a list of citations that support the use of telehealth. I wonder if they have actually read the articles. Here is one citation that I mention only for illustrative purposes. The title of the article posted on an online, not peer-reviewed journal sounds impressive. "The reliability of telepsychiatry for a neuropsychiatric assessment." *Telemedicine and e-Health*. 17(3), 223–225 (Amarendran et al, 2011). Guess the sample size? I bet you did not answer one (1). One subject was evaluated by four raters, of which two were in person and two were remote video. I suspect your threshold of sound science is closer to my perspectives. I am not impressed with the body of research that has been conducted with the specific focus upon assessments. These are ethical issues an evaluator needs to consider (Standard 9.02a).

e. Reporting Findings – this has numerous consequences if not understood. The preemployment examination report is straightforward. Some agencies want the bottom line; is the applicant recommended or not recommended. Other agencies desire a report of history, mental status, integration of testing data and ratings on dimensions that are essential to the performance of duties for the position. The information that may NOT be asked during the interview and included in a report are those prohibited by the Genetic Information Nondiscrimination Act (GINA) Act of 2008 (EEOC, 2008 and 2010).

- You may not ask if a sibling has schizophrenia or a father is an alcoholic. These are prohibited inquiries. The reasoning is because you are conducting the evaluation on behalf of an employer. GINA is specific about what type of health information an employer may gather. GINA impacts all of your evaluations across the continuum referred to in the chart above (see AELE, August 2010.)

Fitness for Duty Evaluation (FFDE)

FFDE or related type evaluations such as Workability Assessments can become problematic. The FFDE is the most contentious evaluation within the specialty of Police and Public Safety Psychology. Others have written extensively on this subject (Corey and Zelig, 2020). The focus of this chapter is not to get into the "weeds" or the merits of even doing the FFDE. It is possible to educate a department to rely on administrative actions and supervisory interventions to the point where the FFDE is a rare occurrence. There are other departments that opt for the FFDE at high rates, in part to avoid administrative actions. Many referrals for the FFDE lack an objective basis. An alternative evaluation, conducted within an occupational medicine framework, may meet the needs of police agencies, reduce the likelihood of adversarial proceedings and lessen complaints against the evaluating psychologist. It is the Workability Evaluation, or Return to Work Evaluation, (Curran, 2014). Health factors, medical and psychological, that limit work attendance or are triggered by specific prescribed medications, FMLA requests, or non-work injury are amenable to the Workability approach rather than a FFDE (Curran, 2014). Educating departments about the benefits about an alternative to the possible job jeopardizing FFDE is ethically responsible, shifts the department to a wellness model of caring for employees and away from an autocratic approach.

"Just because you can does not mean you should."

Case Example: Return to Work – *To Do or Not To Do the FFDE*

This is a composite of the case where a department's dispatcher, police officer, firefighter or other public safety sensitive position has finally heeded advice of family/friends/co-workers and or mental health professional to self-refer to a residential treatment program due to an alcohol use problem. The employer did not refer the employee. The employer had no evidence of problems performing the essential job functions of the position. The employee completed treatment and planned to return to work, when the employer learned directly or indirectly about the alcohol treatment received by the employee. The employer asks that you conduct a fitness for duty evaluation (FFDE) on the employee. The employer affirms that the department's legal counsel has weighed in and supports the FFDE. Before you and the employer are several pathways from which to choose your action. Which from the following is the ethically and responsible action?

A. You decline the request to conduct an evaluation. The basis for declining the referral are multi-factorial.
   You cite to the department that:

1. Americans with Disabilities Act (1990) regulations may apply.
2. You recognize that the department's request has a chilling effect upon employees. The organization's message is that to seek treatment on one's own for a personal matter may cost you your job. You request a meeting with the department's decision-makers to educate them about the benefits of treatment. This includes self-referrals as an important suicide prevention step. You are mindful of APA Ethics codes 1.02 and 1.03 (Conflicts between Ethics and Organizational Demands) and 3.04 (Avoiding Harm).
3. You encourage the department to have the employee return to work and have the chief write a personal note or meet one-on-one congratulating the employee on completing treatment. You encourage the chief to use words that support and sustain the employee's success.

B. You choose to evaluate the employee, even though you are somewhat uneasy about the referral since no job performance deficit nexus exists. Among your considerations are:
   1. The department's attorney agreed with the department to refer. If the attorney says acceptable then I have "cover."
   2. You rely on the case of Brownfield v. City of Yakima since that case is cited by many of your colleagues as providing the rationale for department's not needing to wait for a job problem to occur.
   3. $2,000.00 - $10,000.00 coming your way for doing the evaluation!

Psychologists and other mental health professionals cannot have it both ways. Why? We cannot, on one hand, have a contingent of psychologists mouthing words that encourage departments to institute or grow mental wellness programs, construct and implement suicide prevention programs, and host employee/family functions that foster supporting employees; while on the other hand, engage in potential job jeopardy evaluations on the basis that the department simply can because of safety sensitive position concerns.

An example of where the FFDE is pushed to the limits of acceptability, often in violation of USERRA (1994) is when evaluating returning military service members from activation to a member of the Reserves or National Guard. A fairly broad brush is applied to all mental health professionals to avoid treatment because a small contingent of psychologists is a "hammer" for the department. I have already cited the cell phone confiscation example that exemplifies that just because a department, and their legal counsel, believes they can do something, doesn't make it right. The Supreme Court decision about cell phone confiscation squashed that belief. I encourage psychologists to similarly educate departments away from frequent fitness evaluations. This admonition does not, of course, mean that there may be isolated cases where the fitness examination is ethical, legal and the responsible action.

In addition to the above considerations the following issues are important to review in this chapter. There are a number of pearls I have learned in my career, and two are at the top of the list. First, I learned while consulting with attorneys, psychologists must obtain non-refundable prepayments for any depositions or court appearances. The second was to keep the report of submitted psychological fitness no more than one to two pages. The latter only identifies the reason for referral, records reviewed, diagnostic components and a section for findings that state that the person evaluated was either "fit" or "not fit" for performing the essential elements of the position. Period, nothing more.

You are cringing right now, I can tell. Your generous, kind-hearted, empathic psychologist hat is wanting more, such as recommendations for treatment to either maintain fitness or restore to fitness. Your thought process is understandable but wrong. This topic has been one of the more frequent reasons for exchanges on one listserv for police psychologists. From time to time the question about making recommendations is raised. The response from attorneys has been unequivocal. Do not provide information beyond "fit" or "not fit". I will expand further below but first let's look at more data this author gathered from experienced psychologists.

I describe the table below as an "Arrogance Measure" since more than half of the psychologists surveyed apparently felt they knew best, even better than the employer making the referral. You have not read the 2007 survey question below incorrectly. 54.7% of the psychologists responded they simply did not care what the agency wanted; they were giving more information about recommendations. Let that sink in for a moment. Your client is the agency and not the person evaluated.

If you provide more than a statement of fitness, has the requesting agency asked for more? Or do you fell compelled to provide more information?

	Response %	Response Tally
Agency has specifically requested more recommendations than a statement of fit or not fit.	45.3%	39
No matter what the agency has asked, I will typically provide information about recommendations.	**54.7%**	**47**

It gets somewhat better between the 2007 and a more recent 2016 survey of psychologists. The author re-surveyed psychologists in 2016 and asked the same question. The results (Question #19, below) indicate that fewer suffered from "arrogance" with about 35% compared to about 55% insisting they knew best. A variant to this issue was asked in the 2016 survey where the question about providing a diagnosis was asked (Question #20, below). Again, this is beyond answering the referral question of "fit" or "not fit" to perform essential job functions. Only 40% would not provide a diagnosis. While some psychologists appear to be taking legal admonitions to heart, the remaining outliers as reflected in data from these two questions are concerning. (see 4.04, Minimizing Intrusions on Privacy).

Q19 If you provide more than a statement of fitness has the requesting agency asked for more or do you feel compelled to provide more information?

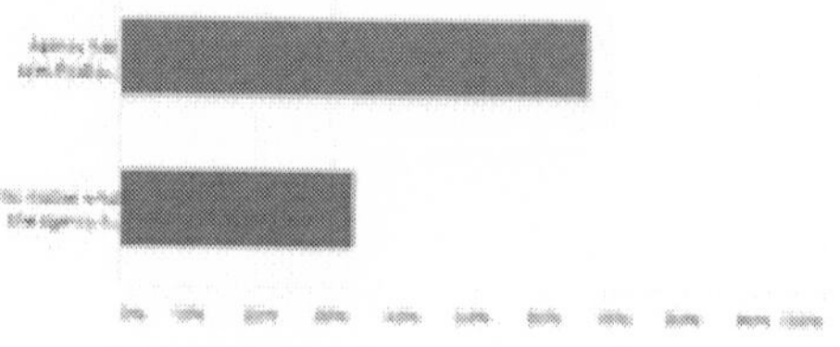

Q20 If you provide more than a statement of fitness for duty do you include information identifying a diagnosis of a psychological disorder?

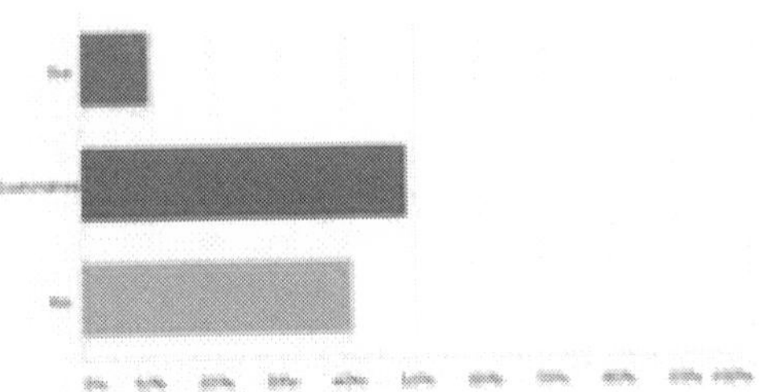

Let's return to examples from questions (composite of postings and paraphrased) posted to a listserv about making recommendations.

Psychologist #1:

> "What are FFDEs for? Clearly, they are first and foremost to establish whether the subjects can fulfill the job requirements and business necessities of the position and do so without danger or damage to self or others. But, in addition, we have a responsibility both to the employer and to the examinee to try to determine whether the person is apt to be capable of restoration to his/her role, in the case where 'unfit' is the conclusion. To simply render a judgment of unfit would, I believe, do a disservice to subject and agency, and, I would argue, could easily lead to charges against the examining psychologist of potential collusion with the department or failure to take the examinees' welfare into account."

Psychologist #2:

> "An employee is now arguing, as part of a malpractice claim, that I entered into a treatment relationship with the employee when I made recommendations in the FFDE report to the Department on potential avenues for restoring the employee's fitness. In this particular employee's case, a recommendation was made in the report for the Department to consider

encouraging the employee to participate in brief individual counseling either through EAP or with a provider of the employee's choosing. We have sought summary judgment on the case, and we are anxious for the result to say the least. It would also seem to me that without making any recommendations, a Department would be left on its own to figure out what to do with an employee rendered unfit."

Here are at least two reasons why the ethical psychologist answers the referral question without, unless asked, any further recommendations.

1. If you are California based, then drilled into your head by now is Pettus v Cole (1994). The case applies to all United States based mental health professionals. Here is a response provided by the late esteemed Martin J. Mayer, an attorney who represented many California police departments. Mr. Mayer wrote in one exchange:

"I would suggest that you check your own state laws regarding compelling an employee to participate in any medical treatment program. In California, we are prohibited from requiring an employee to seek or receive medical treatment as part of the disciplinary process. The case of Pettus v. Cole, 49 Cal App 4th 402 (1996) held that an employer (DuPont) could not compel an employee, who had been diagnosed by the employer's physician as an alcoholic, to participate in a rehab program under penalty of termination from employment. The court ruled that the employee alone is vested with the decision-making process related to his own health care. The employer could only hold him accountable for his behavior as it related to his job. His health choices were his own. Additionally, under California law [Civil Code sec. 56.10, known as the Confidentiality of Medical Information Act (CMIA)], employer's physicians are limited in what information

they can provide to the employer, even when the employee is sent, against his or her will, for a fitness for duty evaluation. Sec. 56.10 states that "No provider of health care shall disclose medical information regarding a patient of the provider without first obtaining an authorization ..." from that patient. The Pettus court held that, despite the fact that he was not receiving treatment from the doctor, Pettus qualified as a "patient" pursuant to the CMIA. The court stated that the CMIA, specifically 56.10(c)(8)(B), "...expressly refers to an employee who is examined by health care provider, at the employer's request and expense, as a 'patient'. Finally, under the Americans with Disabilities Act (ADA, 1990 and 2009), an employer is limited in its ability to make inquiries about an employee's suspected disability and, alcoholism, is a disability."

Mr. Mayer provided further clarity in response to another psychologist's inquiry on this matter. Mr. Mayer wrote:

> *"With all due respects to (Psychologist XYZ), it appears he is unclear on the legal and ethical obligations a retained expert has to his/her client. The duty is to the person/entity retaining you. If, as the retained expert, you take action contrary to the client's wish, you breach your fiduciary duty to the client. If you disagree with what your client wants done, don't accept the assignment or withdraw if it's already begun. As legal counsel to the employer, we have dismissed experts who believed their duty was to the employee. You cannot serve two masters at the same time" (Mayer, 2008).*

2. Another relevant case is Sehie v. City of Aurora, 432 F.3d 749 (7th Cir. 2005), Sehie was a police dispatcher who went home after an incident at work. She then reported to work the next day claiming she left because of an on-

> the-job in jury but was still sent for an FFDE. As a result of the FFDE, the employer required her to attend counseling sessions, and Sehie later claimed the time for traveling to/from and during the sessions to be compensable. The Court of Appeals in the 7th Circuit ultimately agreed and concluded that the purpose of the required counseling sessions was to enable Sehie to perform her job duties and relate to co-workers more effectively and at a higher skill level by addressing personality deficiencies and problems that predated her blow-up at work.

The Sehie case has not been supported in at least one other jurisdiction but remains instructive as why the psychologist needs to address only the referral question.

CHAPTER 7

Counseling/Treatment Dilemmas

The preceding chapters have crystallized for you that:

- You may conduct preemployment evaluations and counseling without inherent ethical binds due to dual relationships;
- You may conduct preemployment evaluations and fitness type assessments for the same department, but not treatment of that department's employees.
- You can almost guarantee opening yourself to ethics complaint vulnerabilities if conducting both fitness assessments and counseling/psychological interventions to the same department.

Providing treatment services to those in high risk occupations is as rewarding as it can get. The client is typically goal oriented, i.e., wants to resolve a personal problem. The client is often quite educated, thus verbal and insightful. Remember, police and emergency services personnel interact with people more often than you probably will ever see. Police, and paramedics in particular, are skilled in assessing people and problems. Also, contrary to stereotypes, clients from public safety agencies are psychologically and physically healthy persons. As a group they are a delight. If you have dedicated your talents to treating this population, you can expect many personal rewards.

Now let's take off the rosy glasses and be aware of the downside some psychologists and other mental health professionals have difficulty resolving. For example, police officers carry guns, and many are required to be armed even when in the therapy session with you. Another downside is remembering how impressed you were with that 23-year-old applicant you saw with military service. Even though he received 50% VA Disability for PTSD, he seemed well suited for police work. Now, five years later, this officer is manifesting an exacerbation of post traumatic stress with anger issues. It is alarming you over his personal safety, as well as the safety of others.

It does not stop there, with a crisis case in your office of a police officer engaged in infidelity, alcohol abuse and facing disciplinary actions for conduct/performance. You realize this is the formula for someone at risk for suicide. Are you going to be able to take the necessary actions that may prevent suicide but possibly contribute to an end to the client's career?

None of these are without successful resolution possibilities. The elements to being successful with this population combine clinical skills with your ethical awareness and sensitivity to being risk aversive. Reaching out to others who have reliably worked with this population is often an alternative, once we get past our ego that we must solve a problem on our own.

I have been fortunate to coordinate a confidential counseling program for a federal agency for 15 years. The program has 300+ mental health professionals of which most are psychologists across the United States. They are much like you if your focus is to a) provide counseling services to high risk occupations as a small percentage (or all) of your clinical hours and b) you do not conduct any fitness oriented assessment services.

My experience has found that the dilemmas that arise in treatment cases are rare. I would have confidence in your skills to apply appropriate decisions if an ethical question arose involving a client working at a high-risk occupation. The problems that may occur are when the psychologist has a direct relationship with an agency to provide services. Some in-house providers have successfully navigated through the potential conflicts. Those in the community may have fewer pressures in their relationship with an agency. Both groups of professionals need to identify potential conflicts ahead of the problem occurring. The experienced professional will more clearly identify that the business ethical organizations with strong decision-making skills are keenly aware of the ethical principles applicable to psychologists. Here is a case example where conflicts may emerge.

Case Example I: Traumatic Event (not an officer involved shooting)

You have become known to one or more departments within your geographic region as reliable source to refer to following a traumatic incident. For example, perhaps a police officer, EMT, or firefighter has been on scene at a car crash with multiple fatalities. Another example is the emergency communications dispatcher who has taken a call from a screaming parent about their toddler who was found drowned in the backyard pool. You have become known as someone who effectively normalizes the acute, albeit normal, intense psychological reactions to these types of incidents. The department has asked you to see one or more of the affected personnel for a one-on-one confidential meeting. You do so and have an initial and at least one follow-up session with the impacted officer/firefighter/EMT/dispatcher/correctional officer. The department representative calls asking if the affected employee is ready (fit) to return to work. Which of the following is the best response?

1. I have a written understanding with the Director of Human Resources (or similar) that provides an outline of what I will and will not provide the department. We have agreed that a one sentence letter is provided to document that the employee was seen on a specified date. No further information is provided.
2. I saw the employee on a specific date for an initial session to process the fatal car crash and then on the specified date again saw the person at which time I administered psychological testing and conducted an assessment of fitness to return to work. Your employee is/is not fit to resume work at this time.

You remain at the head of the class if #1 was your response. Among factors you considered were ethical standards such as:

- 3.11 **Psychological Services Delivered to or Through Organizations**
  (a) Psychologists delivering services to or through organizations provide information beforehand to clients and, when appropriate, those directly affected by the services about (1) the nature and objectives of the services, (2) the intended recipients, (3) which of the individuals are clients, (4) the relationship the psychologist will have with each person and the organization, (5) the probable uses of services provided and information obtained, (6) who will have access to the information, and (7) limits of confidentiality. As soon as feasible, they provide information about the results and conclusions of such services to the appropriate persons.

Further, you considered aspirational guidelines of the IACP Police Psychological Services Section such as:

"In the case of an agency-required intervention, it should include a statement giving the mental health professional limited permission to verify the officer's attendance at the intervention session to the agency without revealing any further details of the intervention." (IACP Officer-Involved Shooting Guidelines, 2018b).

Case Example II: Traumatic Stress Debriefing and Officer Involved Discharge of Weapon

You are the mental health consultant to a peer support team. A group meeting (debriefing) is scheduled for responders to an incident where a person was shot by an officer. The officer involved attends the group meeting. What is your action?

1. You welcome the officer who shot a person to the group meeting and proceed with the debriefing.
2. You immediately escort the officer to a private area and explain that a 1:1 meeting with the officer is appropriate but not the group debriefing.

Choice #2 is the correct answer (there are matters that have black or white, yes or no answers). A few readers may jump out of their chair after reading that #2 is the clear approach. Some will cite state laws and/or regulations that extend confidentiality to group psychological debriefings, or those group and /or the one-on-one meeting led by a peer. I have written about and discussed this ethical dilemma often. It's a case where some minimize the impact of an action by thinking, "I am willing to take that chance."

Let me set the stage with an analogy. Your car has something wrong with the starter and even you, the non-mechanic, suspect something seriously wrong with your vehicle. You take your car to the car dealership since, confident they will know best about your car. The mechanic examines your car and says he found some aspects that were fixable, but the starter is still at risk for further problems. You are the risk aversive car owner who asks, "What type of risks?" The mechanic says possibly one out of a 100 turns of the ignition will result in an explosion. How willing are you at taking that risk? Not very willing? I didn't think so.

Jaffee v. Redmond, No. 95-266[4]

The Supreme Court of the United States ruled in June 1996 that Federal courts must allow psychotherapists and other mental health professionals to refuse to disclose patient records in judicial proceedings. The Court's rule amended Rule 501 of the

4 Among professional experiences was the author's satisfying task of providing content as part of an Amicus Brief on this case.

Federal Rules of Evidence. Why does this matter and who and what was Jaffee and Redmond? Until this decision, the Federal Rules of Evidence *did* recognize privileged communications to psychologists and psychiatrists. The case before the Supreme Court involved a police officer who received counseling following an incident where the officer killed a person in the line of duty. The officer went to counseling with a licensed clinical social worker who refused to disclose the counseling records when those records were subpoenaed by the surviving family of the deceased. Until the Supreme Court rendered its decision, licensed psychotherapists were not covered under Federal Rules of Evidence. Justice Stevens wrote the decision, in which he said, "This case amply demonstrates the importance of allowing individuals to receive confidential counseling. If the privilege were rejected, confidential conversations between psychotherapists and their patients would surely be chilled."

There has been no further Supreme Court decision that extends coverage to non-licensed persons such as peer support personnel; the latter who often are volunteers of fire departments and law enforcement agencies.

Going back to the example, I then pose the ethical dilemma (for some) of allowing an officer to participate in a group debriefing following a critical incident and/or a formal one-on-one debriefing with a peer. Factors that I would encourage you to consider are:

1. Officer involved shootings where someone is seriously injured or killed are more likely than not to lead to litigation citing a violation of civil rights. These cases are heard at the Federal courts.
2. Do you have a duty to protect the officer from participation in an intervention where the peer and other members attending a group debriefing may each be subpoenaed to testify in court proceedings against the officer?

> Your decision, in this author's opinion, is not about how willing you are to take a chance that a federal action will not occur, but rather to take action in the best interests of the officer. We call that nonmaleficence; do no harm. (see Principle A, page 17).

For the above reasons the psychological interventions provided sworn law enforcement personnel are best conducted on a one-on-one basis with a licensed mental health professional. Is there a role for peer support personnel? Absolutely! I, along with Dr. James Janik (Chicago, IL) and the late Dr. Al Benner (San Francisco, CA), had the privilege of drafting the first Peer Support Guidelines of the IACP Police Psychological Services Section. These guidelines were implemented in 1993 under the term of chair, Dr. Nancy Bohl (San Bernardino, CA). Public safety agencies derive many benefits from having competently trained peers (see Chapter 8).

CHAPTER 8

Organizational/Tactical/ Research

In Chapter 3 the four domains and examples of the 57 competencies were listed (page 22). We have already discussed ethical issues worth monitoring related to assessments and when providing interventions. Two domains not yet discussed are those related to Operations and Consulting. Within these domains are 22 areas, of which several are refined elements from Assessment and Intervention. For example, counterintelligence is a component of preemployment assessments and threat assessment is an element of fitness for duty evaluations. The majority of remaining competencies are often within the specialty of Industrial and Organizational (I/O) Psychology.

To the extent that these areas require diligence in maintaining ethical decision making, there are resources that are specific within the specialty of Industrial and Organizational Psychology (SIOP, 2003). Among these is The Ethical Practice of Psychology in Organizations, Second Edition, (Lowman, R, L, (Ed) 2006). The clinically trained psychologist is advised to be ethically aware of competencies prior to engaging in I/O specific roles. A pragmatic rule to follow for the clinical psychologist is the gut check reaction, should an I/O psychologist open a therapy practice down the hall from your office. Competency works both ways!

Competence and Multiple Relationships are the most prominent sources of conflicts when consulting. Clinically trained police psychologists should be alert to these when consulting with organizations. There are plenty of examples where police psychologists favorably impact public safety organizations. These range from the collective guidance about best practices for conducting preemployment evaluations, to fitness for duty to and post-shooting interventions. Also, psychologists regularly contribute to important changes that often go unnoticed by not only the public, but mental health professionals. Take the case of Dr. Lamaurice Gardner (Michigan) changing the HIPAA training throughout the entire Veterans Administration

Health Care System. Here is the background as described by Dr. Gardner (Paraphrased):

> *"I was working with the Sheriff's Office SWAT team as a hostage/crisis negotiator trying to deescalate the emotional upheaval of a barricaded gunman who was a Combat Marine Veteran suffering with PTSD. My efforts to obtain critical clinical information on the veteran through the local VA were shut down by the Emergency Room Physician who stated disclosure would be a HIPAA violation and subsequently hung up on me. The SWAT team members, unfortunately, were eventually forced to engage the veteran and kill him when he came out of his house with a shotgun threatening SWAT operators (Gardner, 2017)."*

The incident fueled Dr. Gardner to pursue all avenues (VA Office of Inspector General and others) to ensure that a similar incident would not re-occur. His determination was recognized as identifying a significant gap in training about Health Information Portability Act and Amendments (HIPAA) throughout the VA Health System. Specifically, a HIPAA covered entity may disclose Personal Health Information (PHI) to law enforcement without the individual's signed HIPAA authorization. The result was a change in policy and training in 2018 at the national level. The entire VA system responded cooperatively to law enforcement requests for information (Gardner, L. 2018). Dr. Gardner's persistence reflected the best in applying ethical principles and standards when confronted with an organizational issue. My challenge to the reader is to be a catalyst for change.

Among areas where little to no change in approach or course content have occurred is entry recruit training and in-service training. This is especially applicable to entry training of aspiring recruits. The reader is encouraged to look at today's academy syllabus and compare to 30+ years ago. Is there an infusion of concepts reflecting best practices of the 21st century? For example, are recruits "trained up" to enhance their emotional intelligence quotient (EQI)? Throughout the past 10 years there has been an infusion of concepts and skills development that lead to improved policing. If your agency has kept current on emerging and best practices, then kudos to those responsible.

Another challenge is to encourage research. What is the nexus between ethical practice and standards? Results from research are central to the ethical practice of police and public safety psychology. The field is wide open for well-designed studies on a variety of topics. Each of the 57 proficiencies referred to earlier would be enhanced by research. How the field of police and public safety psychology reached specialty status by the APA could be debated if research and publications in peer-reviewed journals was a determinant. For example, the APA Division 18 journal, *Psychological Services*, is where the component sections will submit articles for publication. Recall that Division 18 is the diverse Psychologists in Public Service with distinct components that include Veterans Administration Psychologists, Community and State Hospitals, Serious Mental Illness, Health, Indian Affairs, Criminal Justice in addition to Police and Public Safety Psychology. The above journal describes itself as publishing" high-quality, data-based articles on the broad range of psychological services delivered in organized care settings. Specifically, these settings refer to jails, prisons, courts, Indian Health Service, the military, Department of Veterans Affairs, university clinics, training hospitals, and so forth. Note, this description does not even refer to police and public safety!

Here is your last test as we wind down the book.

A review of 6 quarterly publications from 2019 through May 2020 found that 96 articles were published in Psychological

Services. How many of the 96 articles were related to police and public safety?

A. 22
B. 31
C. 2
D. 15

If you chose "C = 2" as the correct answer, then you graduate summa cum laude! The two articles were, *Perceptions of belongingness and social support attenuate PTSD symptom severity among firefighters: A multi-study investigation*, by Stanley et al (2019) and *Agency-offered and officer-utilized suicide prevention and wellness programs: A national study*, by Thoen et al (2020).

The August 2019 Special Issue of *Psychological Services* related to Peer Support, had four articles which, on the surface, suggested relevant findings, but were focused on psychiatric patients and settings. The paucity of peer-reviewed research publications identify the importance for increased research to guide police and public safety practices across all the domains in an ethical manner and cannot be overstated. Too often, mental health professionals base their practices where data is lacking. Here are two prominent examples.

First, Peer Support Programs have grown the past 25 years to the point where workshops for training peers regularly occur and certification status is provided to Peer Support personnel. There is no evidence of effectiveness to these programs. Until well-controlled, random assignment type studies are conducted, the hypothesis that these programs may do harm is an open question. Another example is the focus on training programs to counteract "implicit bias" among public safety personnel, especially police. Do any of these training programs alter behavior?

Mitchell and James (2018) concluded in a Police Chief Magazine article,

> *"The lack of impartial, objective information on the impact of implicit bias training leaves officers, their supervisors, and the public in the dark. Law enforcement training in general is somewhat of a "black box," with very little empirical connection between how officers are trained and how they behave on the street. Regarding implicit bias training, no connection has yet been made between training or training modality and increased fairness in officer decision making behavior."*

Definitive data is imperative to ensure that direction to policies and training are evidence based. An absence of effectiveness data might give us reason to push the "pause" button and reflect upon ethical considerations prior to supporting and expanding our involvement in whichever evolves as the program du jour. We can do better, don't you think?

CHAPTER 9

Consequences and Implications of Biased Policing

Winter to Spring of 2020 was notable for stay-at-home orders due to the COVID-19 virus, a global pandemic impacting millions and causing hundreds of thousands of deaths worldwide. Just as many countries began turning the corner to recovery, a single event in Minneapolis, MN took over every news headline world wide. The incident was the death of George Floyd, a man in police custody. His death has been attributed to the arresting officer's knee placement on the neck of Mr. Floyd. Appropriate citizen protests followed the incident, which days later escalated to civil unrest with violence. In the height of the protests, the American Psychological Association President, Sandra L. Shullman, Ph.D., released a statement to the media on May 29, 2020. In it, Dr. Shullman says,

> *"We are living in a racism pandemic. The deaths of innocent black people targeted specifically because of their race – often by police officers – are both deeply shocking and shockingly routine."*

The use of words "pandemic" and "frequently" are quite powerful. However, is the discussion enhanced by the APA President's use of the above terms? Does the hyperbole blur the important messaging? Have we gotten any better addressing racism problems in law enforcement over the nearly 30 years since the video of Rodney King in Los Angeles? Have we achieved an effective strategy in response to incidents where an officer engages in misconduct where possible race biased policing is in play? I am no expert on the analysis of social problems. However, I do know that if I, a Caucasian male, go to Central Park with binoculars that a woman is unlikely to call the police because of feeling threatened by my presence; that I do not need to take a walk near retail stores holding the hand of a child to reduce my anxiety that if walking alone I might become a target; and have never had fears that my son is at risk of being shot during a routine traffic stop.

The Washington Post examined data from 2015 through 2019 of victims killed by police by race/ethnicity compared to the population of the United States (Washington Post, 2019). This data is powerful in that, as a percentage of the US population, those who are black (12%) are killed by police at statistical rates greater than white persons (26.4% of all those killed). While the raw data of numbers are low, coupled with the limitations of this open source data (Shane and Swenson, 2019)), the occurrence of even one undercuts confidence in the law enforcement institution. I offer my narrow analysis that hopefully serves as going beyond being instructive but contributes to change.

When a U.S. based airliner crashes, does the airline start releasing information a few days post-crash and assure the public that the airline will investigate the cause of the crash? Does an industry where "trust" by the traveling public is essential close ranks when a crash occurs? Please reflect on business ethics as I proceed with this discussion.

The range of the organizational and governmental responses following airline crashes has been planful, organized, tested and transparent. The degree of collaboration among numerous agencies as soon as a plane crashes is not likely fully appreciated by the traveling public. The cornerstone to these steps includes accountability so that re-occurrence is minimized. These steps serve to maintain our confidence. While no 100% guarantee can be provided by an airline, we have confidence in the industry and government that factors related to disregard, incompetence, and cover-up will not contribute to a future crash. Can the same be said for our public safety agencies?

The Tamir Rice Cleveland, Ohio Shooting

On November 22, 2014 Tamir Rice, a 12-year old African American boy, was fatally shot in Cleveland, Ohio by Officer Timothy Loehmann, a 26-year-old police officer. Rice was carrying a replica toy Airsoft gun. Loehmann shot him almost immediately after arriving on the scene. Two officers responded to the scene, having received a dispatch notification that a caller reported a male was pointing "a pistol" out of his pants. The caller stated to dispatch that the gun was probably fake and the person was probably a juvenile. Officer Loehmann and the senior supervising officer, 46-year-old Officer Frank Garmback, responded to the scene. Here are a few facts as subsequently reported:

- The dispatcher did not inform Officers Loehmann and Garmback that the male was probably a juvenile and the gun was probably a fake.
- Officer Garmback did not, per policy, notify dispatch of arrival and did not employ approved tactics upon entering the park where the shooting occurred.

Young Tamir was shot and succumbed to his injuries the next day. The "gun" in his possession was a replica Airsoft gun with the orange tip removed.

Was Officer Loehmann a racist cop? Was he the proverbial bad apple? Probably not. More likely he was psychologically unsuitable for the job and then poorly trained.

Here is some of what the public subsequently learned about Officer Loehmann. He had been with the Cleveland police for less than eight months at the time of the shooting. How did he fare on preemployment psychological testing and background investigation elements? Officer Loehmann had previously worked for another police agency and informed the Cleveland police that he resigned from the prior employer for "personal reasons." After the shooting, the prior employer, the Independence Police Department, (Ohio), reported that Officer

Loehmann was assessed as unfit to be a police officer due to emotional concerns. Officer Loehmann had worked for the Independence Police for five months of which four months were in the academy (2014, Los Angeles Times). The Independence Police allowed Officer Loehmann to resign rather than to be fired. After resigning Officer Loehman applied to another police department but did not pass the initial written test. Neither of these details were reported by Officer Loehman as part of completing an information packet that is used to conduct the background investigation when he applied to the Cleveland Police. Of note, the background investigation that was done by the Cleveland Police did not include reviewing the prior employment file at Independence Police. Officer Loehman was subsequently terminated by the Cleveland Police, not because of the shooting, but because of untruthful statements he made in the application documents.

The Chief of Police for Cleveland is reported to have said the Cleveland Police and the city of Cleveland had learned a lot from the death of Tamir Rice. How much did the department learn? We can infer that the department learned that 6 million dollars of Cleveland taxpayer money was needed to settle the lawsuit filed by the family of the deceased. What we have not learned is anything substantive about the pre-employment psychological evaluation done at either the Independence Police or the Cleveland Police. Further, it is unclear if the Cleveland Police conducted a psychological evaluation. We have not learned about the content of training received related to bias and tactics during the academy training or subsequently through the Cleveland Police. We have not learned about the organizational impacts and changes instituted by the Cleveland Police. There is much we have not learned. Thus, policing moves on to the next wrongful shooting, and the next incident of excessive force leading to death.

What can we learn from other industries that would help cities like Cleveland? Let's return to the airline industry for a moment. Following a crash, here are a few of the actions that we know occur:

- The National Transportation Safety Board (NTSB), an independent federal agency, immediately takes over the investigation - not the airline.
- Release of complete psychological and behavioral analyses profile of flight deck crew.
- Pre-incident crash scene simulation trainings are reviewed. These go beyond training for NTSB investigators. These include airport personnel, airline personnel, firefighters, paramedics, hospital personnel and mental health professionals. There are protocols in place for hotels near departure and arrival airports to host surviving family members.

The above steps just scratch the surface. These actions have served to increase safety for the traveling public, provides immediate interventions by multiple groups, and seamlessly, under high stress conditions, communicate effectively to the public.

In contrast, the steps taken by police agencies following a shooting where an unarmed citizen, especially a black citizen, are investigated as if for the first time for such an occurrence. There is no NTSB equivalent agency that immediately takes over the investigation. Are we long overdue to have a "Police Use of Force Agency," an agency independent from the Department of Justice, whenever any citizen dies as the consequence of police action? Do you think it is unbelievable that there is no consistent collection of data by the FBI, or others, about police involved shootings or related events.? Until the law enforcement community gets out of its own way, consumers will lack confidence that police agencies are concerned about their lives (see sidebar). The civil unrest can be reasonably argued as the direct consequence of police missteps following

Body Camera Recordings Demonstrate Racial Disparites in Officer Respect.

Voigt et al (2017) reported that police officers speak less respectfully to black v. white community members.

officer involved incidents where black lives do not seem to matter. Too many incidents have occurred without any signs of learning how to manage the communication elements to these crises. We need better crisis management to foster, not deter, having support of law enforcement.

Readers of this book, are more likely than not, mental health professionals. However, I hope readers from many public safety disciplines have picked up this book. Regardless, if you are asking what you can do, then let's connect the dots from our principles as listed on pages 15 to 19. Here are a few action steps:

- We can individually educate departments with whom we provide services on a variety of topics that impact enhancing public trust. Review how much the department has altered the recruit training program over the past 30 years. Perhaps the department(s)with whom you consult have not made any significant changes.
- We can demand that our professional organizations take a clear position. Let's each year at professional meetings have a review specifically about police shootings as well as ongoing reviews throughout the year on these incidents.
- Let's finally demand that best professional practices be the standard set by certifying law enforcement authorities such as the Commission on Accreditation of Law Enforcement Agencies (CALEA); and each state's certifying police, cor rections and related public safety commissions.

- Let's prevent a candidate previously determined to be unfit and terminated at one agency to re-appear at another agency without complete disclosure or due diligence regarding prior police performance.

There is even more to do in an ethical and responsible manner than this author has identified. Let's invest in contributing to effective changes.

CHAPTER 10

Summary and Conclusion

Congrats! You made it through the book! Did the content stimulate you to think differently about public safety organizations from a business perspective? Were there clear decisions to ethical problems? Did you learn at least three functions provided by psychologists you may not have previously considered? Did you disagree with at least one opinion offered by the author? If yes, GOOD! Can you defend your position in a mock trial? Can you take the alternative position and challenge your assumptions?

The obstacles are numerous to enhancing 21st century policing, as well as firefighting, emergency services and those related occupations that support public safety. Rarely a day goes by without headline news referring to some aspect of law enforcement actions. Psychologists and others from mental health disciplines bring unique training and perspectives that can impact public safety agencies. These endeavors reflect the best in our principles: do no harm, integrity, trust, responsibility, justice and respect for people's rights and dignity. My hope is that your ethical problem-solving has been enhanced by reading this book. Thank you.

Appendix

Appendix

Assessment Domain

1. Job Analysis
2. Pre-employment, Post-offer psychological evaluations of job candidates
3. Psychological Fitness-for-duty evaluations of incumbents
4. Evaluations for FMLA eligibility
5. Evaluation for reasonable accommodation
6. Evaluations for high risk, high-demand assignments
7. Direct threat assessments
8. Workplace violence assessments
9. Emergency consultations concerning the seriously mentally ill
10. Supervision of psychological assistants, residents, interns, or fellows
11. Pre-offer suitability screening of job applicants (normal traits and competencies
12. Promotional assessments (normal traits and competencies
13. Assessment center development and administration
14. Evaluations (normal traits and competencies) for high-risk, high-demand assignments
15. Psychological autopsies (for purposes other than case resolution)
16. Test development
17. Assessment-related education and training
18. Assessment-related research
19. Assessment-related process improvement
20. Assessment-related consultation Appendix (continued)

Appendix

Intervention Domain

21. Employee assistance counseling
22. Individual therapy or counseling
23. Group, couple or family therapy or counseling
24. Critical Incident early intervention
25. Critical incident therapy or counseling
26. Counseling to cope with unique or chronic job stressors (e.g., deep undercover, homicide, child abuse, etc.)
27. Disability recovery
28. Substance abuse treatment
29. Mental attitude preparation
30. Wellness programs
31. Life coaching
32. Intervention-related education and training
33. Intervention-related research
34. Intervention-related process improvement
35. Intervention-related consultation

Operational Domain

36. Psychological intelligence
37. Criminal profiling
38. Psychological autopsies (intended to facilitate case resolution)
39. Crisis and hostage negotiation
40. Counterterrorism/antiterrorism
41. Counterintelligence
42. Indirect assessment
43. Threat assessments
44. Operations-related education and training
45. Operations-related research

Appendix

Operational Domain (continued)

46. Operations-related process improvement
47. Operations-related consultation

Consulting Domain

48. Development of performance appraisal systems
49. Organizational development
50. Executive consultation
51. Management consultation
52. Supervisor consultation
53. Process consultation
54. Mediation
55. Implementation of multi-rater feedback systems
56. Consulting-related education and training
57. Consulting related research

Appendix from article: Aumiller, G.S., Corey, D., Allen, S., Brewster, J., Cuttler, M., Gupton, H. and Honig, A. (2008). Defining the Field of Police Psychology: Core Domains & Proficiencies. *J Police Crim Psych* 22, 65–76.

References

2010 (8) AELE Mo. L. J. 201 ISSN 1935-0007 Employment Law Section - August 2010. Retrieved from http://aele.org/law/2010all08/2010-08MLJ201.pdf

Amarendran, V., George, A., Gersappe, V., Krishnaswamy, S., & Warren, C. (2011). The reliability of telepsychiatry for a neuropsychiatric assessment. *Telemedicine and e-Health*, 17(3), 223-225. https://doi.org/10.1089/tmj.2010.0144

American Psychological Association. (2013). Guidelines for the practice of telepsychology. American Psychological Association. (2015). Professional practice guidelines: Guidance for developers and users. *American Psychologist*, 70(9), 823–831. https://doi.org/10.1037/a0039644

American Psychological Association. (2016). Revision of Ethical Standard 3.04 of the "Ethical Principles of Psychologists and Code of Conduct" (2002, as amended 2010). *The American Psychologist*, 71(9), 900.

American Psychological Association. (2018). Professional practice guidelines for occupationally mandated psychological evaluations. *The American Psychologist*, 73, 186-197.

American Psychological Association. (2020, May 29). *We are Living in a Racism Pandemic* [Press release]. Retrieved from https://www.apa.org/news/press/releases/2020/05/racism-pademic

Americans With Disabilities Act (ADA) Amendments Act of (2009). 2008. Pub L. 110-325.

Americans With Disabilities (ADA) Act of 1990, 42 US.C

12101 et seq. Pub L. No 101-336. 2.`04 Stat. 328 (1991).

Americans With Disabilities (ADA) Act of 1990, 42 US.C 12101 et seq. Pub L. No 101-336. 2.`04 Stat. 328 (1991).

Anderson, J. (2019, October 23). Baltimore police announce outside investigation into the gun trace task force scandal. *The Baltimore Sun*. Retrieved from https://www.baltimoresun.com/news/crime/bs-md-gttf-outside-investigation-pg-20191023-4rbaav4cwbgejm5ti6xgblf7je-photogallery.html

Arthur, M. B. (2018, September 16). The 'strange history' behind the Myers-Briggs type indicator – And what that can mean for you. *Forbes*. Retrieved from https://www.forbes.com/search/?q=The%20'strange%20history'%20behind%20the%20Myers-Briggs%20type%20%20indicator%20–%20And%20what%20that%20can%20mean%20for%20you.#a831925279f4

Aumiller, G., Corey, D., Allen, S., Brewster, J., Cuttler, M., Gupton, H., & Honig, A. (2008). Defining the field of police psychology: Core domains & proficiencies. *Journal of Police and Criminal Psychology*, 23(1), 48-48. https://doi.org/10.1007/s11896-007-9013-4

Brownfield v City of Yakima, 612 F.3d 1140 (9th Cir. 2010).

Bush, S. S., Connell, M., & Denney, R. L. (2020). Ethical practice in forensic psychology: A guide for mental health professionals. American Psychological Association Commission on Accreditation of Law Enforcement Agencies (CALEA). (2020). Retrieved from https://www.calea.org/

"charlatan." Merriam-Webster.com. 2020. https://www.merriam-webster.com, 2020.

Corey, D. M., & Zelig, M. (2020). Evaluations of Police Suitability and Fitness for Duty. Oxford University Press, USA.

Curran, S.F. (2008, November 9). Results and implications from a 2007 survey of police/forensic psychologists: Fitness for duty assessment procedures. Presentation at the International Association of Chiefs of Police, Police Psychological Services Section, Annual Meeting, San Diego, CA.

Curran, S. F. (2014). Assessment and evaluation: Collecting the requisite building blocks for treatment planning. In *Behind the Badge* (pp. 45-65). Routledge.

Curran, S. F., Blatchley, R. J., & Hanlon, T. E. (1978). The relationship between body buffer zone and violence as assesed by subjective and objective techniques. *Criminal Justice and Behavior*,53-62.https://doi.org/10.1177/009385487800500104

Curran, S., & Savage, C. (1976). Patient response to naltrexone: issues of acceptance, treatment effects, and frequency of administration. *NIDA Research Monograph*, 9, 67-69.

Fenton, J. (2018, June 7). 2 Baltimore police gun trace task force officers sentenced: Jenkins receives 25 years, Taylor gets 8. Retrieved from https://www.baltimoresun.com/news/crime/bs-md-ci-gttf-jenkins-taylor-sentencing-20180606-story.html

Gardner, L. (2017, October 23). Current Issues in Police Psychology. Open Forum at International Association of Chiefs of Police Annual Meeting, Philadelphia, PA.

Gardner, L. (2018, June 14). IACP Psych HIPAA exemption documents [Electronic mailing list message]. Retrieved from a closed listserv psych@mail.iacplist.org.

Genetic Information Nondiscrimination Act (GINA) of 2008. Pub. L. 110-223, 122 Stat. 881 (2008).

Gilbert, C. (2017, December 14). Minimizing mental fitness: Minneapolis police recruits get less psychological testing than they used to. Retrieved from https://www.apmreports.org/story/2017/12/14/minneapolis-police-recruits-psychological-testing

HIPAA Health Insurance Portability and Accountability Act (HIPAA; 1996). Health Insurance Portability and Accountability Act (HIPAA) Security Rule. (2013). Technical safe guards. 45 CFR § 164.312(e), as amended on January 25, 2013.

Hogan, R., & Kurtines, W. (1975). Personological correlates of police effectiveness. *The Journal of Psychology*, 91(2), 289-295. https://doi.org/10.1080/00223980.1975.9923955

International Association of Chiefs of Police (IACP). (2014). Police Psychological Services Section. *Guidelines for pre-employment psychological evaluations*. Arlington, VA: Author.

International Association of Chiefs of Police (IACP). (2018a). Police Psychological Services Section. *Psychological fitness-for-duty evaluation guidelines*. Arlington, VA: Author.

International Association of Chiefs of Police (IACP). (2018b). Police Psychological Services Section. *Officer-involved shooting guidelines*. Arlington, VA: Author.

Jaffee v. Redmond (95-266), 518 U.S. 1 (1996).

Lawson, K. A., Tempelmeyer, T. C., & Hays, J. R. (2020). Ethics for psychologists: Child porn poses ethical dilemma. *The National Psychologist*. Retrieved from https://nationalpsychologist.com/?s=Ethics+for+psychologists++Child+porn++poses+ethical+dilemma

Lowman, R. L. (2006). The ethical practice of psychology in organizations (pp. xvi-303). American Psychological Association.

Luxton, D. D., Pruitt, L. D., & Osenbach, J. E. (2014). Best practices for remote psychological assessment via telehealth technologies. *Professional Psychology: Research and Practice*, 45(1), 27. https://doi.org/10.1037/a0034547

Mai-Duc, C. (2014, December 3). Cleveland officer who killed Tamir Rice had been deemed unfit for duty. *LA Times*. Retrieved from https://www.latimes.com/nation/nationnow/la-na-nn-cleveland-tamir-rice-timothy-loehmann-20141203-story.html

Maryland Board of Examiners of Psychologists (2018, May 17). *In the matter of Kenneth Sachs, Ph.D. respondent before the state board of examiners of psychologists* (Case number 2016-026 & 028). Retrieved from https://health.maryland.gov/psych/Pages/disciplinarya.aspx

Mattis, J. (August 4, 2017). Ethical Standards for All Hands. Memorandum for all Department of Defense Employees, Secretary of Defense, 1000 Defense Pentagon, Washington DC 20301-1000. Retrieved from https://dod.defense.gov/Portals/1/Documents/pubs/Ethical-Standards-for-All-Hands-SecDef-04-Aug-17.pdf

Mayer, M. J. (2008, August 21). FFDE Return-to-Duty Recommendations [Electronic mailing list message]. Retrieved from a closed listserv psych@mail.iacplist.org.

Mitchell, R. J., & James, L. (2018, November 28). Addressing the elephant in the room: The need to evaluate implicit bias training effectiveness for improving fairness in police officer decision-making, *Police Chief Online*.

Pettus v. Cole, 49 Cal. App. 4th 402, 57 Cal. Rptr. 2d 46 (1996).

Reilly, S. & Nichols, M. (2019, October, 17). Prosecutors and police agencies fail to track officer misconduct and frequently circumvent Supreme Court "Brady" rules. *USA Today*. Retrieved from https://www.usatoday.com/

Riley v. California, 134 S. Ct. 2473, 2491 (2014).

Savage, C., Karp, E. G., Curran, S. F., Hanlon, T. E., & McCabe, O. L. (1976). Methadone/LAAM maintenance: a comparison study. *Comprehensive Psychiatry*, 17(3), 415-424. DOI: 10.1016/0010-440X(76)90044-4

Sehie v. City of Aurora, 432 F.3d 749 (7th Cir. 2005).

Shane, J., & Swenson, Z. (2018). Unarmed and dangerous: Patterns of threats by citizens during deadly force encounters with police [Kindle version]. Retrieved from amazon. com

Smith, G. (2016, October 12). The Sports Illustrated cover jinx: Is success a curse? Retrieved from https://www.psychologytoday.com/us/blog/what-the-luck/201610/the-sports-illustrated-cover-jinx.

Society for Industrial, Organizational Psychology (SIOP; US), & American Psychological Association. Division of Industrial-Organizational Psychology. (2003). *Principles for the validation and use of personnel selection procedures.* The Society.

Spilberg, S. W., & Corey, D. M. (2014). Peace officer psychological screening manual. *California Commission on Peace Officer Standards and Training (POST): West Sacramento, CA, USA.*

Stanley, I. H., Hom, M. A., Chu, C., Dougherty, S. P., Gallyer, A. J., Spencer-Thomas, S., Shelef, L., Fruchter, E., Comtois, K. A., Gutierrez, P. M., Sachs-Ericsson, N. J., & Joiner, T. E. (2019). Perceptions of belongingness and so cial support attenuate PTSD symptom severity among fire fighters: A multistudy investigation. *Psychological Services*, 16(4), 543–555. https://doi.org/10.1037/ser0000240

Tayan, B. (2019). The Wells Fargo cross-selling scandal. *Rock Center for Corporate Governance at Stanford University Closer Look Series: Topics, Issues and Controversies in Corporate Governance No. CGRP-62 Version*, 2, 17-1.

Thoen, M. A., Dodson, L. E., Manzo, G., Piña-Watson, B., & Trejos-Castillo, E. (2020). Agency-offered and officer utilized suicide prevention and wellness program: A national study. *Psychological Services*, 17(2), 129-140. https://doi.org/10.1037/ser0000355

Trompetter, P. (2011). Police psychologists: Roles and responsibilities in a law enforcement agency. *The Police Chief*, 78(8), 52.

Uninformed Services Employment and Reemployment Rights Act of 1984 (USERRA), Pub. L. 103-353, 38 U.S.C §§4301-4335 (1994). USERRA Final Rule, 20 C.F.R. Pt. 1002 (2006).

Voigt, R., Camp, N. P., Prabhakaran, V., Hamilton, W. L., Hetey, R. C., Griffiths, C. M., & Eberhardt, J. L. (2017). Language from police body camera footage shows racial dis parities in officer respect. *Proceedings of the National Academy of Sciences*, 114(25), 6521-6526.

Younts, M., (2003). The benefits of psychological testing for preemployment of prospective firefighters in the high point fire department, National Fire Academy Executive Fire Officer Program, North Carolina. https://doi.org/10.1073/pnas.1702413114

Made in the USA
Columbia, SC
19 August 2020